UPSIDE-DOWN & BACKWARDS

THE INNOCENT FAILURE OF
MAINSTREAM PSYCHOLOGY

An Enlightened, Flourishing Life
Via Understanding

The Three Principles That Create Our
Psychological Lives

THOMAS M. KELLEY, Ph.D.

UPSIDE-DOWN & BACKWARDS

ISBN: 979-8-218-06439-6

Cover and Interior Design by
Transcendent Publishing

TRANSCENDENT
publishing

Disclaimer: The content of this book is for informational purposes only and is not intended to diagnose, treat, cure, or prevent any condition or disease. You understand that this book is not intended as a substitute for consultation with a licensed practitioner.

Printed in the United States of America.

Dedication

To my Beautiful Angels—Susan ("My Duck"),
Marty, Kathy, Ricky, Faith, and Michael

Contents

Foreword by Dr. Roger C. Mills ix

PART I:
INTRODUCTION

Chapter 1: Living With the "Mental Flu" and Searching 3

PART II:
MAINSTREAM PSYCHOLOGY

Chapter 2: The Innocent Failure of Mainstream Psychology 13

Chapter 3: Mainstream Psychology's Misdirected "Outside-In/
Something-Missing" Paradigm 25

PART III:
THE THREE PRINCIPLES

Chapter 4: The Three Principles that Create Our
Psychological Lives 39

Chapter 5: Understanding the Power of Thought 59

Chapter 6: Only One Mental Illness 67

Chapter 7: A Path from Three Principles Exposure to
Improved Mental Health 75

PART IV:
UNDERSTANDING THE THREE PRINCIPLES

Chapter 8: Gauging Your Present Level of Understanding the
Three Principles 89

Chapter 9: Some Advantages of Understanding the
Three Principles 99

PART V:
TEACHING THE THREE PRINCIPLES

Chapter 10: Three Principles Mental Health Education 119

Chapter 11: How Three Principles Education Differs from
Mainstream Psychotherapies 129

Chapter 12: Case Examples 141

PART VI:
APPLICATIONS & RESEARCH

Chapter 13: People in Prison for Sexual Violence 157

Chapter 14: School Failure and Delinquency. 165

Chapter 15: Physical Ill-Health: Chronic
Fatigue & Eating Disorders 171

PART VII:
WHEN MAINSTREAM PSYCHOLOGY UNDERSTANDS
THE THREE PRINCIPLES

Chapter 16: Flourishing Mental Health 183

Chapter 17: The Future of Mainstream Psychology 187

Afterword 193

APPENDICES

Appendix 1 : Three Principles Papers, Chapters, and
              Comments Published in Peer-Reviewed
              Academic & Professional Journals, Books,
              and Periodicals (1988-2022) 195

Appendix 2 : Sydney Banks's Books, Audios, and Videos 203

Appendix 3: Three Principles Books, Podcasts, Blogs, and More. . 205

About the Author 207

Acknowledgments 209

Foreword

What follows is (a slightly) updated (by me) version of the Foreword for my first Three Principles-based book, _Falling in Love with Life_. It was written by the late Three Principles pioneer, Dr. Roger Mills. Roger and Dr. George Pransky were the first psychologists to visit Sydney Banks on Salt Spring Island where they were exposed to the Three Principles that create everyone's psychological life experiences. It was an honor to be mentored by Roger Mills. I know in my heart that Roger would approve of my sharing his kind words one more time.

I want to express my gratitude for Tom Kelley's book. Although Tom is a Professor Emeritus of Criminology and Criminal Justice at Wayne State University in Detroit, and a Michigan Licensed Clinical Psychologist, he has never rested on his laurels. He has stayed open and respectful of new ideas. He has not acted as though his accomplishments in the field of psychology and criminology privileged him to feel satisfied or to assume he had all the answers. In 1989, he was exposed to the outcomes of several pilot programs conducted in collaboration with residents of inner-city communities in Miami. In these communities, the Three Principles intervention had been used as the foundation for resident empowerment and community revitalization efforts. Looking as a researcher at the outcomes of these programs, Tom responded with a refreshing openness and insatiable curiosity. He became committed to understanding why these results were far beyond those achieved from other models of empowerment. He observed leadership, motivation, and levels of self-esteem in these communities that he could see would benefit people in all walks of life.

Since then, he has studiously applied himself to grasping the impact and potential of these discoveries for the fields of psychology, criminology, and criminal justice. Although a respected academic and oft published author of professional journal articles, Tom was not satisfied with just an intellectual understanding of new ideas in the field. He sincerely wanted these discoveries to benefit himself, in terms of his own growth and happiness. He realized very deeply the truth of the admonition, "physician heal thyself," recognizing that he could not help others find deeper levels of mental health unless he could see substantive changes in this direction *in his own* psychological functioning. He had the humility and dedication to his field to become a serious student of the Three Principles. Over the last several years, while he studiously applied himself to grasping these Principles, I have come to admire his willingness to question his thinking at every juncture, and to look, from a deeper vantage point, at things that he felt had previously helped him in life.

In addition to the research and case studies used to demonstrate the kinds of changes that result from the logic and power of this approach, Tom was willing to share his own examples. Histories of this own life experiences illustrate how these findings about the nature of our moment-to-moment mental processes can help us all find deeper levels of happiness, and can allow anyone to achieve a wiser, more understanding perspective on life. His willingness to utilize these insights in his life has allowed him to write a book that can assist the reader find what Tom has found for himself.

The Case of Change and Human Nature

The findings reported in this text provide fascinating clues to less personal, broader facts about human nature and change. They offer a more generic understanding of how we all "tick" psychologically. Recognizing these common denominators as factual, as applying across cultures and personality types or lifestyles, automatically triggers a process of personal evolution and change. This process is one that moves us continually toward increased well-being and mature healthy thinking. The discovery of these truths has had the benefit of making the personal growth process more genuine, while less personal, far easier, and more invigorating. Applying these Principles in our personal lives becomes a delightful journey of discovery, one much different than "working on" ourselves. The tone of delight and enthusiasm of this book reflects Tom's excitement of making this discovery, a realization that has now motivated thousands of professionals and researchers to explore and understand these findings more fully.

The True Catalyst for Change

Historically, the early focus in psychology was on identifying pathology and on analyzing past traumas. Therefore, the field of psychology placed more importance on our negative thinking and emotions, on catharsis, on "dealing with" our problems and hang-ups. The discoveries leading to the new Three Principles understanding have shown us just the opposite. The real power for change lies in the direction of deeper, more natural, more forgiving, more gratifying, more compassionate and loving feelings. These qualities of feelings emerge first for us and then toward others as we recognize that we are all in the same boat. These higher quality, deeper feelings; feelings that stem of our innate mental health, are the real catalysts for change. This book points the reader toward both a recognition and unleashing of these qualities of feelings and perceptions.

As Tom points out very clearly in this book, to recognize and benefit from these deeper truths, we must first move away from too much of a focus on our personal thoughts and emotions. Putting these emotions and thoughts in a broader perspective allows change to occur without having to work through all our past, without having to constantly confront or manipulate our thinking or our current difficulties. We can go directly into a healthier way of using the power of Thought that bypasses the disordered personal thinking and affect that got us in trouble in the first place.

The Gift of Thought

As human beings, we were granted the ability to breathe. We have a physical immune system. We can digest food for energy and other natural health maintenance or health enhancing capacities. We were also given the gift of Thought. The explorations leading to the Three Principles understanding convinced us that the gift of Thought is the most powerful capacity of any in our repertoire of inborn faculties as human beings. Understanding how to use this gift in the way it was meant to be used is perhaps the most beneficial outcome anyone could realize from this book.

In our work over the last forty years, these discoveries have been applied across cultures, across diagnoses, and across settings with equally positive outcomes. Our appreciation of the ability of individuals in all walks of life to benefit and change from this understanding was strengthened immensely by the extent of growth in clients of clinical, organizational, and community-based projects conducted over the last forty years. Most people studied in these programs moved from being largely incapacitated, highly dependent clients to becoming healthy, productive citizens. The scope of these results has been amply documented in demonstration programs from Miami to the South Bronx, in Hawaii and throughout the mid-west, to Oakland, CA and South-Central Los Angeles.

The Depth of the Human Potential

This wide variety of applications has shown, in a compelling way, the true depth and promise of the human potential. I am certainly more thrilled and more respectful than ever as the fruits of this understanding multiply and continue to get stronger after forty years. I observe the depth of this potential in everyone because I see it unfolding daily in my work. At times, in this book, what Tom is pointing the reader toward may seem almost too idealistic, unachievable, or unrealistic. I now know with certainty that, at the very least, we all can achieve a relatively stress free, enjoyable, fruitful, and richer life that, at the same time, contributes to the well-being of others. This potential—and much more—exists as a very natural state of mental functioning in all of us. It is always responsive when we realize how to tap into it. Once tapped, it continues to unfold naturally throughout our lives in an almost magical way.

In this book, Tom has presented these ideas and findings in a down to earth manner. His writing style is direct, it is easy to understand, and eminently graspable. As a result, the reader can quickly apprehend the import and usefulness of his ideas. He has been successful at expressing himself in a clear, common-sense fashion. Its purpose is to help people have a nicer, more fulfilling life; to better fulfill their potential as loving, wise, and stable human beings. It will, I am sure, greatly assist readers to find more happiness, vastly reduce stress and live a more rewarding, satisfying, and contented life.

Roger C. Mills, Ph.D.

PART I:

Introduction

CHAPTER 1

Living With the "Mental Flu" and Searching

The following is an updated version of the beginning of my Three Principles-based book, "How Good Can You Stand It!" It best describes my life before and after being exposed to the Three Principles.

I used to be "normal." Like most people, I had gotten so used to living with symptoms of the "mental flu,"—I thought it was normal! For years, I worked to accumulate the "stuff" I thought brought people lasting happiness and peace of mind. I collected a Ph.D., a professorship at a major research university, a thriving psychotherapy practice, an attractive condominium, a shiny red convertible, a pretty girlfriend, and money in the bank. However, after accumulating all the "right stuff," my moments of happiness and contentment were still fleeting.

I did have a great self-image, however. I prided myself on being attractive, intelligent, serious, articulate, ambitious, and successful. Most of the people who knew me as my "image" thought I had it made. Those who knew me better, however, could see beneath the facade. They saw that I was living with a lot of anxiety and self-consciousness that followed me around like my own shadow.

I was "gripped" by these discomforting feelings much of the time. Often, they were attached to my physical appearance or "how I thought I looked." I was compulsive about my hair being perfect. I hated windy days and had favorite check-me-out mirrors in the places I frequented. I hated this lousy habit but couldn't seem to break it.

I also felt a strong urge to prove my worth by outperforming my peers. At one point, I had seven jobs at the same time! I prided myself on this feat. Nonchalantly, I would complain to my friends about balancing these jobs and I assumed they were impressed. Years later, however, I asked some of them what they really thought. Their response was, "We thought you were a little crazy." They were right!

During those crazy days, I woke up most mornings with butterflies in my stomach and a lump in my throat. At social events, I would compare my accomplishments with those of my peers and gauge my place in the pecking order. If I ranked myself below "number one," I would feel depressed and anxious and start searching for a way to climb back on top.

I hunted for potential partners like I was picking out a new car. Partners that satisfied my ego—not my soul. Not long after a relationship began, I would spot some "flaw" in my partner and try to fix it. When one flaw got fixed, I would find another one and work on fixing it. Eventually, my partner would get fed up and "dump me." Then I would feel crushed and try to convince her to stay. When I realized it was "really over," I was depressed for months.

By age 30, I had divorced twice and decided to try some therapy. My therapist was a brilliant man trained in the Neo-Freudian perspective. I typically felt anxious in his reception room waiting for him to open the door to the hallway leading to his office. Eventually, the door opened, and he would nod at me with a faint smile. It was my turn.

Dr. Cowan was formal and serious. He rarely shared anything personal. However, during one memorable session, he exclaimed proudly "I've been doing psychotherapy for ten years and the average burnout time for most therapists is five years!" Yet, he often looked worn out and occasionally became so drowsy he had to struggle to keep his eyes open.

During therapy we focused on my childhood and family dynamics. We analyzed my insecure feelings, dreams, divorces, and compulsive habits. We did this weekly for about eighteen months. Our sessions were intense, and I typically felt anxious while we talked. I was afraid that some awful part of my personality was going to suddenly show up and scare the heck out of me!

I felt somewhat better after therapy—less compulsive and perfectionistic—more self-confident. Yet, I had little understanding of the source of this improvement and how to sustain it. More importantly, I still wasn't where I wanted to be. I still didn't have the understandings necessary to experience well-being as a way of life.

During and after therapy, I was a self-help book junkie. Most of the books I picked were grounded in the cognitive-behavioral therapy (CBT) perspective. CBT challenged the prevailing notion that people's feelings and perceptions are caused by their circumstances, situations, and how other people treat them. Instead, CBT proposed that people's feelings are caused by their beliefs about the events, circumstances, and people in their lives.

For me, there was something helpful in this new perspective. I spent considerable time—as these books suggested—uncovering, challenging, and refuting my irrational beliefs. I worked diligently at trying to think more rationally and began using CBT in my private practice. However, while the tools and techniques of CBT made a difference for me, something was still missing. For example, when I was in a low mood, I found it difficult to work at thinking more rationally. During my down times, I didn't feel much like challenging my biased beliefs. While the thought reconditioning tools of CBT helped me cope with my insecure moods and painful feelings, I still wasn't spending much time feeling exhilarated, content, and fulfilled. Some important understandings were still missing.

The following summer, I was perusing the self-help section at another bookstore. I ended up buying a paperback that described a controversial group training that was quite popular at the time. While reading this book, I had an insight. I realized that I was spending much of my life being "an impostor." It occurred to me that I had made up a story about me and my life that I thought was "the truth." It dawned on me that I was living most of my life as a character in a make-believe story I had concocted in my own mind!

Anxious to deepen this new insight, I enrolled in the next available training. Back then, these trainings were held in hotel ballrooms. I can't remember the hotel, but I'll never forget what happened the evening before the first training day. Shortly after checking in, I noticed three cold sores erupting on my lower lip. You can imagine how this went over for a guy who thought his appearance had to be flawless. In the morning, I would enter a brightly lit hotel ballroom with around two hundred strangers—WITH THREE HUGE COLD SORES! After a mild panic attack, I rushed to a nearby drugstore and bought the strongest over the counter cold sore ointment I could find. Back in my hotel room, I basted those critters most of the night. The medicine hardly fazed them!

The next morning, I invented a way to camouflage the cold sores with a skin-colored Band-Aid. Fortunately, even I had enough sense to realize that the Band-Aid was more conspicuous than the blisters. Finally, I self-consciously dragged myself to the training room—nonchalantly covering my mouth with my hand and avoiding direct eye contact with nearby trainees. Hey, I did the best I could! Anyway, as the training proceeded, I forgot about the cold sores and started feeling my "normal" again.

Our trainer was extremely confrontational. He berated us—lectured incessantly—put us through several closed-eyed processes—had intense interactions with participants who were brave enough to raise their hand. Some of his techniques were pretty strange. For example, we had to imagine rappelling down the inside wall of a giant strawberry! Initially, many trainees were frightened, confused, bored—even outraged.

By the end of the second weekend, however, some striking transformations seemed to occur for many participants. Several trainees appeared to experience marked improvements in their mental health. Some seemed to make more progress in just two weekends than most of my "successful" psychotherapy clients after months—even years—of therapy! For example, several trainees contacted their parents, siblings, children, and ex-spouses, telling them how much they loved them and apologizing for past hurts, betrayals, and abuses. Others appeared to let go of grudges they had kept alive for five, ten, twenty—even thirty years! In just two weekends, many participants appeared to put their pasts back in the past and resolve long-held complaints, problems, issues, grudges, and resentments.

The rapid and dramatic improvement in mental health that seemed to occur for me, and many other trainees led me to question many of my core beliefs about how people work psychologically and how they change. Yet, I had no idea how the training worked. For the life of me, I couldn't figure out the source of the bursts of mental health that I and many other trainees experienced.

Following the training, I participated in several seminars available to graduates. While I got value from these classes, a confusing thing happened. I began drifting back into my old anxious feelings and compulsive habits. Not as intense as before, perhaps, but still annoying and perplexing. I figured that I must have lost "something" I had gained from the training. By participating in more seminars, I hoped to find "it" again. Occasionally, the well-being and vitality I experienced following the training returned. Soon, however, these healthy experiences would fade away. To my dismay, something was still missing. I still didn't have the realizations necessary to sustain this health as a way of life!

My Missing Breakthrough

The following spring—guess where I was? That's right—in the self-help section at another bookstore searching for something to read on a flight to Florida. I spotted a title that intrigued me—*Sanity, Insanity, and Common Sense.* This ground-breaking book offered a new explanation of the way people's psychological lives are created. It was my first exposure to a new understanding that today is commonly known as the "Three Principles." I'm not sure why, but I realized then that these three simple Principles represented a paradigm shift—a true breakthrough for the fields of psychology and psychiatry!

The Three Principles explained the source of every feeling and state of mind I had ever experienced. They clarified why at times I got stuck in anger and resentment and how, at other times, I felt compassion, respect, and love for everyone. These Principles accounted for the times I became defensive, irrational, and emotionally unstable as well as my hopeful, inspired, and creative moments. They made sense of my every behavior, from the most foolish and self-destructive to the wisest. The most complex human problems and experiences appeared to be explained by the logic of these Principles! More importantly, this new understanding helped me see that everyone has all the mental health they need already inside them!

I began teaching the Three Principles to my therapy clients. The clients who grasped a sufficient understanding of the Principles moved from merely coping with life's challenges to responding to them with more ease and contentment. They often saw their own wise—often creative solutions—to their problems. The Three Principles also became the major focus of my university research and teaching. I soon noticed heightened interest and enthusiasm from my students. For example, many of my criminology students began seeing the innocence in the health-damaging behavior of people engulfed in the criminal justice system. They began relating less personally to the misguided actions of these people. I began writing papers that applied the logic of the Three Principles understanding to at-risk youth, delinquency, criminality, trauma, domestic violence, and child abuse and neglect. My vision for reducing these and other social problems skyrocketed!

Via grasping a sufficient understanding of the Three Principles, I finally realized how we all work psychologically. I saw how I slowly drifted away from my mental health birthright and became "normal"—another human being living with symptoms of the "mental flu" and searching for a cure. The Three Principles guided me to these new insights in a gentle, compassionate way. No confrontation, no gimmicks, no New Age malarkey, no struggle, no tools, no techniques, no willpower—NO COLD SORES!

Via a sufficient insight-based understanding of the Three Principles, I saw that everyone can realize and sustain mental well-being as a lifestyle. These new insights allowed me to think "like a kid" again and experience more of the joy, exhilaration, and spontaneity I typically experienced as a young child. And you know what—I haven't visited the self-help section of a bookstore *to get better* since!

Update

We live in a world in which most people are in a state of spiritual starvation. Old understandings must give way to new ones if our world is going to flourish rather than regress and deteriorate. The source of a flourishing life lies within you, not out there. A flourishing life is not sourced by what you do, but what you are. A sufficient understanding of the Three Principles will awaken your consciousness of your True Self and create a climate in which you will flourish, experience a system of Oneness, and meld your mind with the consciousness of Infinite Intelligence.

Over 25 years have passed since I wrote the above! During that time, I have had the privilege to author and/or co-author over 40 Three Principles-based empirical studies, theoretical papers, chapters, and comments all published in respected peer-refereed academic and professional journals, books, and periodicals. However, I'm not done yet! My intuition recently nudged me to put it all together—to write another Three Principles-based book that: a) describes the innocent failure of mainstream psychology and its misdirected "outside-in/something-missing" paradigm; b) explains how the Three Principles "inside-out/nothing-missing" paradigm can ignite mainstream psychology's transformation from a splintered, tinkering field, with separate and often competing theories, practices, and areas of specialization—*to a true science*, c) combines Three Principles mental health education with supportive empirical research evidence, case examples, and Three Principles-based YouTube videos and podcasts; and d) illuminates a path to a more upright, enlightened, flourishing life.

What follows combines selected and updated material from my Three Principles-based papers, empirical studies, chapters, comments, and books in a way that will hopefully assist readers to deepen their understanding of the Principles of Universal Mind, Consciousness, and Thought. Following each chapter, is "**A DEEPER DIVE**" where I cite Three Principles-based videos, podcasts, and/or additional writings and videos that can assist readers to grasp a deeper understanding of the material presented in that chapter. Before we begin our journey together, please reflect on the wise words of Jonathan Marshall:

"A teacher can only lead you so far and hope that you will have courage to pause and look within and find that wisdom already present in your own consciousness. That wisdom, will then lead you to love, understanding, and contentment—to peace, harmony, and healing of your distress."

Tom Kelley, Ph.D.

PART II:

Mainstream Psychology

CHAPTER 2

The Innocent Failure Of Mainstream Psychology

Here we are, whirling around the sun and sailing through the universe. In less than a century, we have conquered many once-fatal diseases, landed men on the moon, sent a rover to Mars, created flying cars, and are on our way to constructing hotels in outer space! Most of us live in climate-controlled homes, eat foods imported from far away lands, live decades longer than our ancestors, exchange messages via email and texts that used to take days for delivery, and live material lives that make Renaissance kings look like beggars. Yet far too often we become so emersed in stress, depression, and anxiety that we seem oblivious to our wealth of luxuries and experience little satisfaction in living.

When we become stressed, depressed, or anxious, some of us look for help from therapists. Others attempt to heighten their state of mind via meditation, prayer, exercise, diet and rest, the company of friends and family—or perhaps alcohol, cannabis, or antidepressants. However, the prevailing therapies and myriad strategies we use to improve our mental health are typically far from optimal, short-lived in effectiveness, and may have health-damaging downsides. The bottom line—mental ill-health is skyrocketing worldwide, and very few adults are *genuinely mentally healthy or flourishing!*

The Striking Rise in Mental Ill-Health

Millions of people currently suffer from a mental or neurological disorder. Over 75% of people in the world will be affected by these conditions at some point in their lives. The numbers are staggering and are expected to cost the global economy $16 trillion by 2030! In the U.S., except for cardiovascular disease and physical rehabilitation, mental ill-health is the costliest medical condition—over $225 billion a year. For major depression alone, the direct and indirect costs are estimated at more than $50 billion. Before the onset of the COVID-19 pandemic in 2020, about 1 in 12 U.S. adults had a diagnosis of depression. During the pandemic, however, those numbers rose to 1 in 3 adults! This sharp rise likely explains why in 2020, almost $27 billion worth of antidepressant medications were used across the globe.

Regarding adolescents, depression rates have more than doubled in recent years with 15% of these youth reporting at least one depressive episode in the last 12 months. The Youth Risk Behavior Surveillance System (YRBSS) reported that 37% of high school aged students experienced persistent feelings of sadness or hopelessness during the past year, 19% of high school students had seriously considered attempting suicide, and 9% had attempted suicide one or more times! African American youth under the age of 12 are twice as likely to die by suicide than their white counterparts. Latinx adolescents are also at an increased risk, with young Latinx women twice as likely to attempt suicide as white teens. For Asian American young adults between the ages of 15 to 24, suicide is now the leading cause of death.

Mental illnesses are also a major cause of the number of years of life lost prematurely to death and the number of years lived with disability. Mental ill-health is a leading cause of disability-adjusted life years, second only to coronary artery disease. However, is a population that lives long but is in poor health better off than one with a shorter but healthier life span?

The Gradual Decline in People's Mental Health

Mental health research points to a gradual decline in people's mental health from childhood to midlife and beyond. Grace Kent and A. J. Rosanoff stated:

"No sharp distinction can be drawn between mental health and mental disease; a large collection of material shows a gradual and not an abrupt transition from the normal state to pathological states."

Psychologist, Corey Keyes, administered a set of well-being items to 1,234 youth ages 12–18. Based on their responses, Keyes classified these youth as flourishing (38%), moderately mentally healthy (56%), or languishing (6%). Flourishing was the most common category among youth ages 12–14 (49%). However, moderate mental health was the most prevalent category among youth ages 15–18 (52% moderate: 40% flourishing). Keyes's findings have been replicated in several national and international studies. In sum, by late adolescence, the mental health of most people is far from flourishing. Even more striking, as adolescents age into adulthood, the percentage of flourishing declines even more. According to Keyes, "Very few adults… could be classified as genuinely mentally healthy—*less than 2 in 10 adults (17%) were completely mentally healthy.*"

In another study, psychologist, Avshelom Caspi and his associates, followed 1,037 people from ages 3 to 45. During this 42-year interval, psychiatric disorders and brain images were assessed 9 times, starting at age 11. By midlife (age 47), 86% of the cohort met the criteria for a mental health disorder at some point in their life. The onset of disorder occurred by adolescence for 59% of participants! The researchers concluded "… *people who sustain enduring mental health are rare exceptions (14% in our cohort)!*"

Anything Less than Flourishing is Hazardous

Considerable research shows that anything less than flourishing mental health is associated with increased disability and burden to self and society. According to Corey Keyes, flourishing adults function superior to all others in terms of the fewest workdays missed, the lowest level of health limitations, the fewest chronic physical diseases, the lowest health care utilization, the highest level of psychosocial functioning, the lowest level of perceived helplessness (low perceived control in life), the highest level of functional goals (knowing what they want from life), the highest level of resilience, and the highest level of intimacy (feeling very close with family and friends). Compared to flourishing mental health, adults with moderate mental health exhibit substantial impairment. Moderate mental health is associated with high limitations of daily living, more reductions in work productivity, more chronic physical diseases, and poorer psychosocial functioning. In sum, Keyes stated:

> "… If almost there is good enough, the current approach to national mental health is succeeding, because approximately one-half of the adult population is moderately mentally healthy. However, because genuine mental health should be the goal, the current approach to national mental health is a failure, because only 17% of adults are completely mentally healthy!"

Coping Strategies and Psychotropic Medications

Mainstream psychology's massive use of coping strategies and psychotropic drugs has largely failed to reduce the prevalence of mental ill-health. For example, the global prevalence of major depressive disorder and anxiety disorders has remained steady over that last 30 years. Among the more problematic issues, researchers point to the "chemical imbalance" theory of depression, which has helped create a boom in antidepressant drugs meant to modulate certain chemicals in the brain called neurotransmitters. A large meta-analysis of antidepressant trials concluded that antidepressants had almost the same effect as a sugar pill and that their widespread use has not delivered measurable results. For example, in the U.S. alone, antidepressant use increased by 352% from 1990 to 2020—yet there has been *no observed reduction in the prevalence of mood, anxiety, or substance use disorders in any Western country!* Anthropologist, Kristen Syme, lead author of a paper published in the *Yearbook of Physical Anthropology* stated "Only treating the 'psychic pain' with coping skills and drugs does not solve the underlying problem. It's like medicating someone for a broken bone without setting the bone itself." Evolutionary anthropologist, Edward Hagen, added:

> "Mental health research is still very much stuck in a view that comes out of the 19th century, and revived in 1980, of classifying everything by symptoms in the hopes of revealing underlying patterns that would lead to solutions, but it really has not… Even though we're using new measurements, like genetics, biomarkers, and imaging, these still haven't added up to the insights needed to really improve people's lives."

Burned Out Psychologists and Failed Interventions

Even more striking, the mental health of most mainstream psychotherapists is far from optimal. Up to 78% of psychologists and psychiatrists suffer from emotional, physical, and spiritual burnout—many within five years of starting their practices! Furthermore, the effectiveness of the interventions used by these professionals is typically far from optimal. A comprehensive study of the efficacy of mainstream psychotherapies showed that, on average, their effectiveness was smaller than initially reported and often nil. Voluminous outcome studies have attempted to determine the percentage of psychotherapy participants that sustain their goals in therapy at 6-, 12-, 18-, and 24-months following treatment. Several meta-analyses of these studies report reasonably encouraging success rates at 6- and 12-month intervals. However, these studies consistently show these success rates falling dismally at 18- and 24-months after treatment. Consider the following statement by psychiatrist, Thomas Insel, following 13 years as Director of the National Institute of Mental Health:

"When I look at the number of suicides, the number of disabilities, the mortality data, it's abysmal and it's not getting better. All the ways we've approached these illnesses, and with a lot of people working very hard, the outcomes we have gotten to this point are pretty bleak."

Failed Replications

Replication of mainstream psychology's research studies is a fundamental aspect of normal science. A survey of 1,500 scientists published in the journal *Nature* reported that 24% said they had published a successful replication and 13% had published an unsuccessful replication. Contrast this with over a century of mainstream psychology publications, *where just 1% of papers attempted to replicate past findings*!

The OSC Reproducibility Project—in the largest crowdsourced effort to date—270 investigators attempted to replicate 100 studies published in 3 major psychology journals. Ninety-seven of these 100 studies initially reported statistically significant findings. However, only 36% of the replications did so with a mean effect size (the importance of the difference between the control and experimental groups) of less than half of that reported in the original studies. In this regard, sociologist, Thomas Scheff, noted that over the past 50 years more than 20,000 studies have used some 200 self-esteem scales. Their failure, he said *"...is clear; the scales ability to predict behavior is less than 5%!"*

Doctored Research

Other questionable research practices include ceasing to collect data when a study starts showing the suspected results and using statistical methods most likely to show significance. Data transparency is another common problem—researchers are seldom required to submit their raw data for peer review and many researchers are reluctant to make this data available when asked to do so. Also, mainstream psychology journals are unlikely to publish research papers with non-significant findings—findings that show no difference between the control and experimental groups. Thus, studies with significant positive findings are overreported, creating a biased perception of treatment efficacy. Finally, researchers tend to exaggerate the meaning of small effect sizes—making minor effects seem larger than they are.

In a survey of 2,000 American psychologists, some 67% admitted selectively reporting studies that "worked," while 74% failed to report all measures they had used. The survey also found that 71% continued to collect data until a significant result was obtained, 54% reported unexpected findings as if they were expected, and 58% excluded data after analyses. Incredibly, *more than one-third admitted they had doubts about the integrity of their own research on at least one occasion and 1.7% admitted to having faked their data*!

Perpetuation of Individualism

Individualism is prized by Western society—doing what is one's own best interest with less concern for others or the larger society. Therefore, it should be no surprise that mainstream psychotherapies also promote individualism. Consider the following targets of these interventions—*self*-concept, *self*-realization, *self*-esteem, *self*-empowerment, *self*-affirmations, *self*-awareness, and the rigorous examination of one's *personal* thoughts! While there is value for some to focus on these individual goals, there are also downsides. One major downside is the current infestation of entitlement—that one is entitled to certain necessities, resources, and privileges without having to earn them. Psychologists, Kevin Glenn and M. Paul McCormick, described it this way:

> "It includes a "Me! Me! Me! mentality" of "I want! I want! I want!" It is an exaggerated self-love… reminiscent of narcissistic personality disorder. Surely… not all people… fall into extreme categories. However, the goals of mainstream modalities align with the criteria for entitlement, and indeed individualism… One need not look far to see citizens destroying their communities, to see violence, students in schools… defying local law enforcement, special interest groups promoting unconditional respect and diplomatic treatment of citizens regardless of their behavior, teenagers and young adults disobeying their parents, school rules, and the law… Values such as work ethic, pride in ownership, delaying gratification, earning and accepting one's lot in life, and personal accountability become lost within individualism, leading to an embellished sense of entitlement."

Gus Speth, US Advisor on climate change and Yale professor, put it this way:

> "I used to think that top environmental problems were biodiversity loss, ecosystem collapse and climate change. I thought that thirty years of good science could address these problems. I was wrong. The top environmental problems are selfishness, greed, and apathy, and to deal with these we need a cultural and spiritual transformation and we scientists don't know how to do that…"

The Failure of "Evidenced-Based" Psychotherapies

As a result of rigid insurance regulations and parity laws, evidence-based psychotherapies (or EBPs) are considered "the most effective." There is also considerable pressure from these powerful entities to mechanize the therapy process. Each session is pre-planned—the therapist is required to stick to a pre-determined agenda—with no space for therapist wisdom, creativity, and adjustment. Also, the mechanical laboratory-constructed format differs from the varied ways practitioners in the field deliver the same therapy. It would be impossible to study every therapist's personal approach to administering these therapies. Thus, it is highly unlikely that EBPs will show the same effectiveness in the field as they supposedly show in the laboratory. Kevin Glenn and M. Paul McCormick put it this way:

> "The upshot of these EBPs is that they stand as a monument to psychotherapeutic failures: failure to relate meaningfully to the client, failure to fully conceptualize a client's suffering, failure to develop appropriate and comprehensive interventions, failure to provide clients with sufficient options for transformation, and failure to help the client to the full potential of which we are capable. Even the therapeutic interventions themselves in the most ideal of conditions frequently result in failure. But this is what happens when science becomes the primary guide of psychotherapeutic interventions…"

Theoretical Issues

In a paper published in the prestigious journal, *American Psychologist*, Christopher Ferguson cites several issues within mainstream psychology that he asserts have "sullied its reputation and credibility." Ferguson emphasizes mainstream psychology's replication crisis, particularly the defensiveness of researchers regarding this important issue. He further highlights psychology's mechanistic view of people—particularly its "… overemphasis of the power of modeling and reinforcement on people's behavior and its minimization of people's complexity, free will, and wisdom."

Another problem is the tendency of researchers to attach their reputation to their prized theories and to protect those theories by sacrificing scientific rigor. This is particularly true for theories and research funded by powerful advocacy and political organizations. Researchers supported by these powerful groups may compromise research standards via searching for or emphasizing findings that support the beliefs and goals of these organizations. The consequence, according to Ferguson, "… the line between science and advocacy is often blurred leading to confirmation bias and scientific inbreeding."

In sum, the problems associated with mainstream psychology are longstanding, with researchers, reviewers, editors, journals, and news-media all prioritizing and benefiting from the search for novelty and funding. This systemic bias, along with little consensus on *fundamental Principles* in mainstream psychology, means that dubious research practices can flourish—consciously or unconsciously. Psychologist William Doherty summed it up this way:

"After 45 years of doing therapy, I know one thing for sure, and that's that I don't know much for sure. I used to think that we therapists knew, or would soon discover, the underlying causes of psychological and relational problems. Scratch that hope: we have as many explanatory models and inconclusive studies today as ever. I also used to think that my favorite treatment model would become the silver bullet for thorny treatment issues—or at least clear the field of most competitors. But nope: we still have no evidence that any one treatment model is more effective than others for the vast majority of problems we see in therapy. Okay, but at least most of us practitioners get a bit better with time and experience, right? Alas, available research shows that on average, therapists don't have better client outcomes over time, even if we feel more confident in our work as we gain experience."

A DEEPER DIVE

There are several excellent speakers and teachers of the understandings that we will visit in this book. So, following each chapter, I cite Three Principles-based YouTube videos and/or podcasts produced by some of these teachers. Occasionally, I will also cite some non-3P videos. I'm confident that these wise words will assist you to grasp a deeper understanding, via insight, of the material presented in each chapter.

On YouTube please watch:

Dangers of Modern Psychology: Fr. Ripperger (38-minute version)

Why an Entire Field of Psychology is in Trouble?

Limits of Scientific Psychology/Nick Brown

Calling Bullshit 7.4: A Replication Crisis

7 Flying Cars that Actually Fly

CHAPTER 3

Mainstream Psychology's Misdirected "Outside-In/Something-Missing" Paradigm

What's going on here? What's wrong with this picture? Why is the effectiveness of mainstream psychotherapies so small, so short-lived, or even zilch? Why do so many mainstream mental health professionals burnout so quickly? Why do most of mainstream psychology's prominent research studies fail to replicate? Why do an increasing number of young people believe that death is an easier alternative to life? Why are mainstream psychology's theories, models, studies, and therapies failing to assist so many people to realize and sustain flourishing mental health?

Mainstream psychology certainly didn't plan for or expect these dismal outcomes. What is it that mainstream psychology is missing that could ignite its transformation from a splintered, tinkering field, with separate and often competing theories, practices, and areas of specialization—*to a true science*? Is mainstream psychology ready to explore plausible alternatives that could have an enormous impact not only on policy, but on the lives of mental health practitioners and the clients they serve? What is a contemplative, well-meaning mental health practitioner to do?

On the other hand, what if mainstream psychology is doing the very best it can based on the misdirected paradigm through which it views the way people's psychological lives are created? Mainstream psychology's prevailing view is that people's psychological experiences (e.g., feelings, perceptions, moods, symptoms, etc.) are created primarily *from the "outside-in"—via the events and circumstances they encounter and how other people treat them.* Mainstream psychology commonly promotes the misguided notion that people's discomforting symptoms and self-defeating behaviors are, for the most part, attributable to social, cultural, political, and economic factors, and the actions of others. With few exceptions, mainstream psychology views mental health through an *"outside-in/something-missing"* lens—that mental ill-health is caused by outside events and missing external factors (e.g., coping strategies, meaningful activities, religious affiliation, rational beliefs, intimate relationships). On the other hand, what if these external factors are of marginal importance compared to people's inner lives whereby, with only minor prompting from external sources, people often churn up anger, resentment, envy, greed, jealousy, and hatred?

This "outside-in/something-missing" paradigm fails to explain several facts such as why people exposed to the same circumstances show very different outcomes. For example, poverty is associated with family and community breakdown. However, many poor families stay together and raise successful children. Marital distress is associated with poor problem-solving skills. However, many couples who are poor problem solvers are content and stay together. On average, people exposed to four or more forms of adverse childhood experiences (e.g., abuse, neglect, bullying) have a lifespan shortened by around 20 years! On the other hand, many others exposed to similar adverse events during childhood lead long, healthy lives. Trauma researcher, Dean Simonton, stated:

> "… it is a startling testimony to the adaptive powers of the human mind that some of the most adverse childhoods can give birth to the most creative adults. On the other hand, many children raised in a decent, loving manner are prone to believe they are somehow wronged or damaged."

Mainstream psychology also views mental health from this "outside-in/something-missing perspective. It typically sees mental health as a commodity that must be "put into" people from the "outside-in" via assisting them to change their circumstances, alter their relationships, recondition their beliefs, take on new beliefs, and learn and persistently practice myriad tools, techniques, and coping strategies. For example, to improve their clients' mental health, psychiatrists Giovanni Fava and Jenny Guidi advocate the use of "well-being therapy," which promotes self-observation, the use of a structured diary, homework, taking on positive beliefs (e.g., life has purpose and meaning), and developing skills to promote satisfying relationships, effective life management, and self-efficacy. Cognitive-behavior therapy or CBT attempts to teach people various skills, techniques, and new beliefs and behaviors designed to help them change their attitudes, challenge dysfunctional thoughts, resolve conflicts, solve problems, and manage negative emotions. On the other hand, many people who religiously practice these techniques are not flourishing and others who have never heard of these techniques are. Is offering people coping strategies, techniques, and psychotropic drugs the best that mainstream psychology can do to assist people to handle the stress it posits as an inescapable consequence of life?

How This "Outside-In/Something-Missing" Paradigm Evolved

Before World War II, psychology appeared to be headed in the direction envisioned by one of its principal founders, Willian James. During its early years, the bulk of psychology's writings and research focused on mental health and uncovering *Principles* that could guide people to more fulfilling lives. This goal was exemplified by the early writings of John B. Watson on effective parenting, Carl Jung's work on the meaning of life, and Lewis Terman's research on giftedness. Following the War, however, two major events sidetracked psychology from this noble mission. First, in 1946, the Veterans Administration was established and immediately offered psychologists vast amounts of funding to better understand and treat *mental illness*. Second, in 1947, the National Institute of Mental Health was born and offered psychologists lucrative grants to research *mental dysfunction*. The unfortunate result—psychology's focus quickly shifted away from promoting mental health to better understanding and treating *mental ill-health*. Renown psychologist, Abraham Maslow, lamented "It is as if psychology has restricted itself to only half its rightful jurisdiction, and that, the darker, meaner half." Martin Seligman added:

> "We became a victimology. Human beings were seen as passive foci; stimuli came on and elicited 'responses,' or external 'reinforcements' weakened or strengthened 'responses,' or conflicts from childhood pushed the person around. Viewing the human being as essentially passive, psychologists treated mental illness within a theoretical framework of repairing damaged habits, damaged drives, damaged childhoods, damaged brains."

Almost eight decades have passed since these events transpired. However, mainstream psychology continues to focus primarily on dysfunction, weakness, and impairment. Psychological treatment continues to focus primarily on symptoms and repairing damage within a disease model of human functioning.

The Birth of Positive Psychology

During the 1990's, several prominent psychologists called for mainstream psychology to reduce its emphasis on dysfunction and rekindle its long-neglected mission of making people stronger and more productive and actualizing high human potential. In 1998, Martin Seligman, President of the American Psychological Association, called for a Manhattan Project for psychology. Seligman asserted that psychology must look beyond human weakness and damage and reclaim its fundamental mission—*understanding human strength and virtue*. In response to Seligman's call, *positive psychology* was born in 2000. Its mission—*the scientific study of human strength, resilience, and optimal human functioning.*

Since its beginning, positive psychology has developed scores of models and carried out thousands of studies to better understand and facilitate human well-being and resilience. Interestingly, in the 2006 inaugural issue of the *Journal of Positive Psychology*, P. Alex Linley, Steven Joseph, Sue Harrington, and Alex Wood expressed the same aspiration for positive psychology that William James envisioned for traditional psychology:

> "Looking into the future, our aspiration would be that positive psychologists may even be able to discover principles that unite different conceptions of the positive and good, thus allowing movement toward a taxonomic understanding of positive psychological phenomena that would provide a meta-theoretical foundation for optimal human experience."

The Same Misdirected "Outside-In/Something-Missing" Paradigm!

Unfortunately, positive psychology grounded its models, research, and interventions in the same misdirected "outside-in/something-missing" paradigm as mainstream, disfunction-focused psychology. For example, prominent positive psychologists David Myers, Mihalyi Csikszentmihalyi, and Edward Diener asserted that happiness and "the good life" are tied to myriad external forces such as the quality of one's work and leisure experiences, a supportive network of close relationships, religious faith, intimate marriages, and realistic goals. Reed Larson argued that positive attributes like altruism and self-efficacy are connected to participation in carefully structured positive activities and organizations. George Valliant proposed that increased social supports, interpersonal safety, rest, nutrition, and sobriety are essential to transmute less adaptive defenses into more adaptive ones. David Buss posited that well-being can be enhanced by increasing the closeness of extended kin, developing deep friendships, selecting a mate with similar values, and managing competitive mechanisms. Peter Salovey postulated that emotional and physical health can be improved by increasing desirable life events, avoiding the suppression of positive and negative feelings, working through and/or managing negative emotions, and changing and correcting one's environment.

Most of the very early proponents of a more positive psychology were also entrenched in this "outside-in/something-missing" view. For example, Abraham Maslow's self-actualization, Jack Block's ego-resiliency, Ed Diener's positive emotionality, Aaron Antonovsky's salutogenic approach, Julius Seeman's personality integration, Edward Deci and Richard Ryan's autonomy, Charles Scheier and Michael Carver's dispositional optimism, Mihalyi Csikszentmihalyi's flow, and Martin Seligman's learned optimism all posited that certain external in-puts improve the quality of life. These include cognitive restructuring, altering negative attributions, engaging in meaningful activities, satisfying lower need states, and changing attitudes and perceptual styles—all necessary to restructure people's goals and subsequently improve the quality of their psychological lives.

Living an "Outside-In/Something-Missing" Life

On day one of my classes at Wayne State University, I often ask my students the following question: "Can anyone tell me the source or cause of every psychological experience that people can have (feelings, perceptions, states of mind, etc.)?" Astonishingly, not one student has offered the correct answer! Their typical "outside-in" responses—past and present circumstances, socialization, temperament, environment, personality, and heredity.

What's even more striking—most mainstream mental health professionals can't accurately answer this question! This liability explains why, at last count, there were over 400 different psychotherapies—each with a different view of the source of people's psychological experiences—each with a different approach to prevention and treatment! Please consider the chances of getting your "sick" car running smoothly again if there were over 400 different views on how to repair the exact same engine!

Why is it essential to understand the way that you, me, and everyone else work psychologically? Well, how about this? If you don't understand how something works, how can you use it in your best interest? If you don't realize how something works, how are you going to fix it if it breaks down? If you don't know how something works, are you not more likely to misuse it and innocently hurt yourself?

The "More, Better, Different" Game

When people don't understand the way that their own (and everyone else's) psychological experiences are created, they innocently live in the illusion that the quality of their psychological lives depends on "stuff out there"—their possessions, accomplishments, circumstances, and how other people treat them. They typically believe that their feelings, perceptions, and states of mind are created from the "outside-in." When people don't realize how they (and everyone else) work psychologically, they tend to view "stuff out there" as the major source of the quality of their psychological lives.

What happens next? Well, when people believe that the quality of their psychological lives depends on "stuff out there," they spend a lot of time attending to and tinkering with "stuff out there." They become attached to what I call the "more/better/different" game. People think that the "good life" depends on collecting *more* "stuff out there" (e.g., money), getting *better* at "stuff out there" (e.g., parenting), and doing different "stuff out there" (e.g., get married, make a baby).

Playing "more/better/different," can never transport people to sustained mental well-being. Most people don't realize this, however. Why? Because most people don't understand the way they (and everyone else) work psychologically—that flourishing mental health doesn't come from "stuff out there." So, when their first round of "more/better/different" tinkering doesn't lead to sustained well-being—they try again. In the next round, they collect *more* stuff, get *better* at stuff they're already doing, or try *different* stuff.

Can you blame people for being seduced by the "more/better/different" game? Of course not! When people lack a sufficient understanding of the way people's psychological lives are created, it really appears to them that flourishing mental health can be realized and sustained by accumulating the right "stuff out there." Even when their inner wisdom tries to warn them that they are looking in the wrong direction for the source of flourishing, most people don't trust their intuition even when it smacks them directly "on the noggin." Not trusting their inner wisdom and witnessing countless others hooked on the "more/better/different" game, most people think, "What if my intuition is wrong and my friends find more happiness (i.e., stuff) than me?" Thus, most people keep searching and searching—playing "more/better/different" over and over—never sustaining the mental well-being they crave. Instead, most people spend big chunks of their lives tinkering with the stuff they've collected and stored in their "outside-in" caverns!

The Need for Universal Principles

In his wonderful book, **Prevention from the Inside-Out** (available on Amazon), Jack Pransky offered the following historical perspective regarding the need for Universal Principles. While shifting psychology's emphasis back to its original goal of better understanding and facilitating mental well-being was long overdue, positive psychology has failed to uncover and adopt *Principles* that explain the way every person's psychological life is created. Instead, positive psychology adopted the same misdirected "something-missing/outside-in" paradigm as dysfunction-focused mainstream psychology. Absent the direction of a Principle-based foundation, positive psychology (like mainstream psychology) has splintered into separate, often conflicting theories, models, and areas of specialization, each with its own research agenda based on its own cherished set of variables. Thus, positive psychology's efforts to learn and evolve continue to be done separately and simultaneously, rather than systematically and in concert. Without Universal Principles that account for everyone's psychological experiences and behaviors, any explanation of the "good life" is as possible and feasible as any other. Only Universal Principles can bring true discipline to positive and mainstream psychology and provide a consistent standard upon which to judge the truth and integrity of their findings, propositions, and interventions. Only a psychology grounded in *Universal Principles* can lead to a genuine transformation in people's mental health.

In 1891, William James expressed the need for psychology to discover *Universal Principles* that represent true human nature. By Universal Principles, James meant *general scientific laws that explain how something works and have numerous special applications across a wide field.* The direction James suggested for the then-emerging field offered clues to where such Principles might be found. For example, James stated, "The only thing which psychology has a right to postulate at the outset is the *fact of thinking* itself." James also linked thought inseparably to *consciousness* and postulated, among other things, that:

> "Every thought tends to be part of a personal consciousness; Within each personal consciousness, thought is always changing; Within each personal consciousness, thought is sensibly continuous... The consciousness of Self involves a changeable stream of thought... although [that], at each moment, [is] different from that of the last moment..."

James also considered the "spiritual self" and saw its link to thought as follows:

> "Our considering the spiritual self at all is a reflective process, is our abandoning the outward-looking point of view, and of our having become able to think... of ourselves as thinkers... We can feel, alongside of the thing known, the thought of it going on as an altogether separate act and operation in the mind."

James saw this "spiritual self" connected to what he called "*Absolute mind...* the essence of which we know nothing."

With such statements, James, perhaps unbeknownst to himself, pointed in the direction of a trinity of Principles behind the psycho-spiritual nature of life—*Thought, Consciousness, and Absolute Mind.* Though unable to be examined by the human eye or later by the microscope, PET, or MRI, the belief that people are composed of both spirit (psyche) and matter (soma) has been broadly accepted for centuries. Psyche is the Greek word representing the spiritual (i.e., formless) aspect of humanity often designated as Mind, Soul, or the "Breath of Life." Psychology originally was the science or study of the soul or mind. However, unable to measure it within the scientific method, psychology abandoned the exploration of the psyche and focused primarily on biology and behavior. Behavior and biology have lent themselves far more easily to observation, measurement, and research than do life, mind, and soul. However, what if looking in the direction of the psyche holds answers that have heretofore been elusive, even if initially it does not appear easy to measure, research, or even grasp?

Despite James's pleas to the field, what became mainstream psychology did not appear to notice or embrace these Principles, their interrelationships, or their relationship to human behavior. Mainstream and positive psychology have yet to discover, recognize, and approve such Principles. However, until they realize and adopt a Principle-based foundation to guide their understanding of the way people's psychological lives are created—MAINSTREAM AND POSITIVE PSYCHOLOGY WILL CONTINUE TO (INNOCENTLY) HAVE IT UPSIDE-DOWN AND BACKWARDS! The consequence—mainstream and positive psychology's efforts to assist people to steer clear of psychopathology and its symptoms and to realize and sustain flourishing mental health will continue to bear small fruit!

Yet, what if Universal Principles really exist that explain the true nature and source of all human psychological experiences? Moreover, what if those Principles also provide the heretofore-elusive link between psychology and spirituality? Finally, what if a sufficient understanding of these Principles can empower people to live a more RIGHTSIDE-UP, ENLIGHTENED, FLOURISHING LIFE! The purpose of this book is to examine these questions and posit an answer.

A DEEPER DIVE

On YouTube watch:

How Simple Ideas Lead to Scientific Discoveries

William James: The Psychology of Possibility: His Life and Contributions to the Field of Psychology

The History of Positive Psychology: The Science of Human Well-Being

Positive Psychology Introduction: Research, Theory, Criticisms

PART III

The Three Principles

CHAPTER 4

The Three Principles That Create Our Psychological Lives

Everything that exists and happens in the universe is a perfect expression of *Principles—fundamental truths, laws, or facts of nature that explain how something works, or why something happens.* Principles that explain the way everything works are constantly operating—continually "doing their thing"—whether people realize it or not. Principles are impersonal. For example, it makes no difference to the Principles behind a tsunami if hundreds of people lounging on a beach get swept away. The Principles behind electricity and gravity don't care if someone who doesn't understand them gets electrocuted or slips off the edge of the Grand Canyon. It is immaterial to the Principles that create our psychological lives if we don't understand them, innocently misuse them, and suffer from chronic mental stress.

Throughout history, the biggest breakthroughs for humanity have occurred when someone uncovers Principles. When someone realizes Principles—shares their realization with the world—the world is eventually transformed. When Principles are uncovered, understood, and adopted, people finally realize the way things created by these Principles "really work" and are empowered to use the Principles in their best interest. When people "catch on" to Principles, there is an explosion— a vertical leap—of positive change in the domain operated by those

Principles. For example, people's life spans have increased dramatically because Principles behind the operation of the human body have been uncovered. Fewer people are killed or injured by tornados, hurricanes, and tidal waves because scientists better understand the Principles that spawn these events and are better able to predict their location, celerity, and intensity. Electric-powered vehicles and flying cars now exist and the International Space Station orbits Earth because science has grasped a deep understanding of the Principles behind electricity and gravity.

The Three Principles

In 1973, Sydney Banks, an ordinary laborer residing on Salt Spring Island in British Columbia, Canada, experienced a "spontaneous spiritual transformation" during which he realized that Three Principles which he eventually referred to as *Universal Mind, Consciousness, and Thought*, account for people's entire psychological life experiences and behaviors. One of the founding community psychologists and cofounder of the *Journal of Primary Prevention*, Donald Klein, a mentor of prevention pioneer Jack Pransky, described Banks's transformation as follows:

"Several years ago, the director of a community mental health center in Oregon... suggested I look into the positive effects on people's physical and emotional well-being being achieved by a spiritually enlightened man in British Columbia. A few years before, this man... had suddenly entered into a vastly different level of awareness, a form of spontaneous spiritual transformation about which William James had written in the early 1900's... It was obvious this man had achieved a state of understanding and grace, based on no particular religious philosophy or practice... his discoveries... were obviously worth exploring from the standpoint of preventive mental health... something very important was taking place... our most basic assumptions about human behavior were being challenged."

Sydney Banks asserted that Universal Mind, Consciousness, and Thought represent fundamental truths always operating in the psychological realm, much as gravity exists as a Principle of the physical world and is always present, whether people know of it or not. Banks asserted that these Three Principles represent the unifying, undergirding Principles for psychology that William James originally envisioned but never fully realized! Banks stated:

> "…You have to have the power of Mind and you have to be Conscious and you have Thought to relate to your life. Anything else is a product of their usage. Therefore, it is virtually impossible to think of any mental activity that isn't a product of the Principles."

The Principle of Universal Mind

What is the fundamental truth of Universal Mind? Banks (1998) referred to Universal Mind as "… the intelligence of all things whether in form or formless… [and he asserted that] Universal Mind holds the secret to all psychological functioning." Universal Mind points to the fact that the universe is intelligent; that there would be no creative forces in the universe, nothing living, if not for an intelligent life force or energy. Banks saw Universal Mind (or Mind) as the formless energy that animates all of life—the intelligent life energy or life force that powers people's psychological functioning. Banks stated:

> "There is only one Universal Mind common to all, and wherever you are it is with you always… constant and unchangeable… The personal mind is in a perpetual state of change. Universal Mind and personal mind are not two minds thinking differently, but two ways of using the same mind… All humans have the ability to synchronize their personal mind with the impersonal Mind to bring harmony into their lives."

Some physical analogies are helpful to clarify the nature of Universal Mind. For example, physiologists tell us that our organs are powered by a force beyond themselves: a life force that science has yet to measure. Physicians assert that a brain by itself does not function, a heart does not beat, and a nerve does not fire. Rather, our organs make use of a formless life energy and, in so doing, our body accesses a profound natural intelligence. Mechanical equipment (e.g., an electrical cord and outlet) receive and conduct the power of electricity which physicists tell us is also generated by an intelligent formless energy. In a similar fashion, the power behind our ability to have thoughts, and then experience those thoughts "as real" through our senses, is the same intelligent formless energy that powers physical life and mechanical equipment.

A DEEPER DIVE

On YouTube watch:

Sydney Banks and the Three Principles

Big Little Mind with Sydney Banks

The Principle of Mind with Judy Sedgeman

The Missing Link Chapter 4 - Mind with Bill Pettit & Judy Sedgeman

Introducing the Three Principles: Michael Neill

The Principle of Universal Consciousness

What is the fundamental truth of Universal Consciousness? Universal Consciousness points to the fact that people must somehow be conscious of life, or they would have no experience of it—that without Consciousness, people would be unaware of their own existence or anything that happens within it or to it. Banks asserted, "Universal Consciousness... enables us to observe and experience the existence and workings of the world we live in." On a personal level, consciousness animates our thoughts via our physical senses, which creates our moment-to-moment psychological life experiences. Banks referred to personal consciousness as "… the gift of awareness … [which] allows for the recognition of form, form being the expression of Thought."

Banks also distinguished levels of consciousness stating:

> … as our consciousness descends, we lose our feelings of love and understanding and experience a world of emptiness, bewilderment, and despair. As our consciousness ascends, we regain purity of Thought and, in turn, regain our feelings of love and understanding.

Banks asserted, counter to mainstream psychology's prevailing "something-missing/outside-in" paradigm, that "Mental health lies within the consciousness of all human beings, but it is shrouded and held prisoner by our own erroneous thoughts." In this regard, the problems for which people seek psychotherapy are the result of experiencing and/or behaving in response to the "reality" they see at lower levels of consciousness. Each level looks and feels very real at the time, but it is only "real" when one sees it from that level of consciousness, and the level through which one sees the world can change at any moment with their next thought. Banks asserted that with incremental insights, one's level of consciousness increases and one's experience of the world changes.

A DEEPER DIVE

On YouTube watch:

The Principle of Consciousness with Judy Sedgeman

The Missing Link Chapter 5 - Consciousness with Bill Pettit & Judy Sedgeman

The Principle of Universal Thought

What is the fundamental truth of Universal Thought? Universal Thought points to the fact that every person has the power to create thoughts. Banks stated,

> "Thought is the creative agent we use to direct us through life." People can use the power of Thought in infinite ways; to create happiness or sadness, forgiveness or anger, exhilaration or depression, and everything in between… Thought is the master key that opens the world of reality to all living creatures… Thought is not reality, but it is through thought that our realities are created."

Thought, as a Principle, does not refer to people's already-formed thoughts or the products of people's thoughts (e.g., feelings, perceptions, moods, beliefs, symptoms). Rather, the Principle of Thought refers to the fact that everyone is continually "using" the power of Thought to create the thoughts that—enlivened via consciousness— become their psychological experiences. When Sydney Banks asserted that everyone "uses" the power of Thought, he was not suggesting that people "do something"—that tools, techniques, or strategies are necessary. Rather, he meant that everyone continually uses the power of Thought to have psychological experiences in the same way everyone constantly uses gravity to stay anchored to Earth. In other words, people are the thinkers of their thoughts and the creators of their own perceptions of external events and experiences. Judy Sedgeman stated, "When we look out into the world, we are making up what we make of it; *the world is not forcing us to make up one thing or another.*" Regarding people's behavior, prevention specialist, Jack Pransky added:

> "What we have missed [in prevention], in my view, is this: We have forgotten, or ignored, or not realized where behavior comes from. All behavior arises from thought. No matter what

wonderful things we do in the name of prevention or health promotion, unless people's thinking changes, their behavior will not change. Our behavior always follows our thinking. This is an irrefutable fact one only has to reflect on to see its truth."

The Three Principles appear to work together in the following way: something happens in the outside world; for instance, people find themselves in various circumstances and situations and are subjected to what other people do to them. Then the creative power of Thought generates some thoughts about what happened, which is instantaneously picked up by their consciousness and impinges upon their senses to produce a perception and/or feeling. Thought is always what makes us see the world the way we do, and consciousness always makes that way of seeing it look "real" to us. People do not often recognize this; nor do they often realize that as the "reality" they see (through thought) shifts, their thinking, feelings, and actions change accordingly. Nor do they typically see that when they are lost or absorbed in some activity, their mental health improves. The system is inexorable; the only experience people can have is their own thoughts coming into their consciousness and being experienced as "real" at various levels. In sum, what Banks realized is how everyone creates "reality" the same way via their use of these Three Universal Principles and, therefore, how everyone creates a different or "separate reality" moment-to-moment!

A DEEPER DIVE

On YouTube watch:

The Principle of Thought with Judy Sedgeman

The Missing Link Chapter 6 – Thought (Part 1 & Part 2) with Bill Pettit & Judy Sedgeman

Innate Mental Health

Sydney Banks realized further that well-being, resilience, and wisdom exist within the core or essence of all people via pure consciousness—consciousness uncontaminated by personal or conceptual thoughts—which serves, figuratively, as a direct access to Universal Mind. In other words, at our core, we are all mentally healthy (i.e., nothing-missing) and we can realize and sustain this health throughout life because this health is our natural state—our spiritual essence. Jack Pransky described it this way:

> "At the essence of our consciousness, uncontaminated by personal thoughts, is the pure energy of Universal Mind, manifesting within every human being as a natural state of mental health… When people have thoughts that arise from this innate health… they experience feelings of well-being. This [innate health] is also the incubator… for new insights of wisdom to rise from out of the blue. This healthy state of mind can only be contaminated to varying degrees by people's innocent misuse of the power of Thought."

In sum, people can experience only two ways of being—either they are operating from innate mental health, or they are obscuring this health to varying degrees by their own personal thoughts. Three Principles psychologist George Pransky put it this way:

> "The Three Principles suggest that innate health is available to all people, always, as a way of life. [This health] is a birthright [that] provides the feelings that people want for themselves. It provides a transcendent intelligence for problem solving. It provides an uncontaminated view of life to enjoy the moment… [It] is free from chronic stress and distress. It enables people's humanity to come through in their personal relationships. [This innate health] is the most undiscovered and unappreciated resource in human existence!"

Young Children are Great Examples

Young children typically live in innate mental health without any training, techniques, or coping strategies. Young children are not awake in the middle of the night trying to figure out how to handle life. Young children don't give a hoot about improving their "self-image." They haven't yet learned to connect their self-worth with their thoughts, feelings, accomplishments, beliefs, traits, and other "stuff out there." They typically wake up feeling exhilarated, have boundless energy, absorb knowledge like little sponges, express themselves fully, show love and affection unconditionally, dance, sing, act unselfconsciously, and typically rebound from discomforting states of mind in no time flat. Young children spend most of their time fully present in the moment—*thinking at the speed of life.*

A DEEPER DIVE

On YouTube watch:

Sydney Banks – The Great Illusion

The Missing Link Chapter 13 - Wisdom with Bill Pettit & Judy Sedgeman (2 parts)

The Three Principles Explained: Your Guide to Innate Health: Life Hacks

Innate Health - Eliminating Stress & Creating a Healthy Community #1

Feelings: A Reliable Gauge of the Quality of Our Thoughts

Banks further asserted "Our feelings are the barometer of our thoughts." In other words, *our feelings are a reliable gauge of the quality of our thoughts, informing us when we are operating from our "innate mental health" or obscuring this health to varying degrees with our own personal thoughts.* While we may not often realize what we are thinking in the moment, discomforting feelings signal that our thoughts are not serving us well. The more painful our feelings, the more disordered our thoughts.

Once people realize that painful feelings are brought about and sustained by their own personal thoughts, they find it increasingly easy to dismiss those thoughts. In other words, using the signal of a discomforting feeling to discern that their thinking is skewed or off-kilter, people can quiet down and allow the discomforting thoughts to pass through. George Pransky stated:

> "… Feelings are reliable guideposts to [the quality of our] moment-to-moment thinking and registering on them serves the purpose of awakening us to the present use of the [power of Thought] and pointing us beyond this use to the underlying Principles."

That's right—negative, painful, insecure emotions won't build your character—make you a better person—add to your appreciation of positive feelings—build up inside of you—spoil or damage you. You don't have to "get in touch with them" or "get them out" to feel better! All of these ideas are NONSENSE! Roger Mills put it this way:

> "Negative emotions are not stored up like air in a balloon or pus in an abscess; they are not forced upon us from the outside but are created moment to moment by people's thinking. If clients realized this, they could begin to drop their insecure [thoughts] that keep negative emotions in place and begin to find mental health and more loving feelings. Trying to achieve mental health via negativity is like trying to achieve peace of mind through fighting. It can never be done."

More Wonderful Examples of Young Children

I'll never forget the day I observed some children at a friend's daycare center. For about an hour, I risked being in the same space with a dozen or so toddlers. The first thing I noticed was that each child was fully present—completely absorbed in their play and learning activities—curious, involved, spontaneous, and *very* self-expressive!

Every so often, however, the state of mind of one child or another would suddenly shift. For example, Jimmy became angry and snatched a toy from a playmate. Susie started crying and ran to a teacher. Robbie stomped off to a corner and sulked. Brandon knocked over another boy's Lego sculpture. However, these sudden shifts in mood were very short-lived. Each one lasted a few seconds to perhaps a few minutes. Each discomforting mood ended almost as abruptly as it began. With a little TLC or distraction from a teacher, each child moved back into healthy gear—fully immersed in their activities again as if nothing ever happened!

What accounts for this behavior? Most young children are fully present in the now—effortlessly guided by their innate health (i.e., Universal Mind). Now and then, however, a discomforting thought comes down the steam—enters their mind—and they hold it in place. Consider Susie, for example, the little girl who started crying and ran to a teacher. The thought that Susie kept "squeezing" was, *Billy pinched me.* Sobbing profusely, Susie must have repeated this to her teacher ten times— Billy pinched me! Billy pinched me! Billy pinched me! Susie tenaciously held on to this discomforting thought—allowing it to stagnate in her mind. However, with a little loving attention from a teacher, Susie quickly let it go—her innate health re-surfaced—and Susie was back in the flow. For young children, discomforting moods are like summer thunderstorms. They happen occasionally—are part of their natural "psychological weather"—are typically brief—quickly forgotten—followed by the sunshine of innate mental health.

I left that daycare center thinking how different life would be for us "older kids" if we continued to relate to our discomforting thought storms in the same way we did as young children. As adults, the time we spend obscuring our innate health would be much less indeed! During our discomforting "thought attacks," we wouldn't take our thoughts to heart and keep "squeezing them" like stubborn pit bulls. Much sooner we would be back in the flow—Universal Mind at the helm—basking in well-being, gratitude, and exhilaration.

So, what happened? Why, as we grew older, did we stop relating to our discomforting personal thoughts in the way we typically did as young children? Why, as we added years, did we start feeding or entertaining discomforting thoughts and "buying in" to the painful reality illusions they spawn? Why, as time went by, did we begin using the creative power of Thought against ourselves and chronically obscuring our innate mental health for hours, days, months—even years? Why on earth would we do this to ourselves?

Here's how it looks to me. As time passed, most of us *innocently* learned to misuse the power of Thought. *I can't emphasize enough that this was innocent!* Why? Because nobody ever told us or our peers and caregivers—whose misuses of Thought we modeled and that they reinforced—about the Three Principles, the power of Thought, and the power of innate mental health!

Thinking Like a Kid Again

My client, Don, was depressed and angry after being fired from a high-paying job. Don made a mistake judging the potential of a business his company purchased based on his research and recommendation. The business went "belly up" and Don got fired. Don was so gripped by depressive thoughts that it was difficult for him to even look for another job. He spent most days watching TV and playing solitaire. For some reason, during our first session, I proposed to Don "a way to find a wise solution for his predicament." Here's what came out of my mouth:

> "Don, how about we go out to my waiting room or down the street to the elementary school and see if we can spot a young

child. If we find one who is willing to assist us, you can describe your situation to the child. However, you have to state just "the facts." Then, you can ask the child for a possible remedy."

To my surprise, Don took me up on my proposal! He "lightened up" and said, "Okay, let's try it." Fortunately, my next client that day arrived early and was accompanied by her five-year-old son, Jeremy. I had met Jeremy before, and he seemed happy and outgoing. Don and I headed from my office to the waiting area, and I introduced Don to Jeremy and his mom. Don asked Jeremy if he could ask his opinion about a problem. Jeremy was eager to help and, with mom's approval, the three of us proceeded back to my office.

Just the presence of this beaming, enthusiastic child raised Don's spirits. Jeremy was ready to play and spontaneously asked Don, "What's your problem?" Don did quite well sticking to "just the facts."

Don: Well Jeremy, I had this job I really liked. I made a lot of money. I also made a big mistake and my boss fired me. Now, I'm sad and depressed. I'm not sure what to do.

Jeremy: Did you tell your boss you were sorry and ask him to take you back?

Don: I did. But he said no.

Jeremy: I think you should find a nicer boss to work for.

Don: Actually, Jeremy, he was a good boss. I just made a big, dumb, stupid mistake.

Jeremy: Well, that's okay. Everybody makes mistakes. My mom says mistakes are good because you learn new things.

Don: I know, but I should have known better. I was really stupid.

Jeremy: It's okay to do dumb things. I do them all the time. Just apologize, forget about it, and find a new job.

Don: You are probably right Jeremy... but it's not that easy.

Jeremy: You seem nice and smart to me. How many jobs have you asked for?

Don: Well, none yet.

Jeremy: Then how do you know it's hard?

I think you all get the idea. Jeremy was guided by his innate wisdom. At one time or another, we have all been "blown away" by the striking clarity and common sense of a young child's view of life. With their personal thoughts and biased beliefs seldom obscuring their innate wisdom, young children are masters at seeing life's obvious and sensible possibilities. Through the lens of pure consciousness—a simple, sensible solution for Don's "problem" was obvious to Jeremy. No big deal!

Don, however, had drifted away from his innate health. He was trapped in discomforting thoughts, painful feelings, and distorted perceptions—desperately searching for a way out. However, with insufficient understanding of the Three Principles, it was difficult for Don to stop "spinning his wheels" and allow his innate wisdom (i.e., Universal Mind) to guide him.

A DEEPER DIVE

On YouTube watch:

Why Do We Break Down Mentally with Bill Pettit.

Innate Evolution: The Psychological Immune System Video.

Innate Evolution: The Weather of Our Minds.

The Best Kept Secret in Well-Being: Jack Pransky

The Missing Link Chapter 11 - Feelings with Bill Pettit & Judy Sedgeman

All Feelings Including the Good Ones Come from Thought – An Audio with Valda Monroe

Principles Don't Care if People Understand Them!

Please imagine that you visit your local hardware store and buy an electrical wiring kit. If you understand and follow the instructions to the letter—wire things up in sync with the Principle behind electricity—the lights will shine—the buzzers will buzz—everything will work perfectly. On the other hand, if you misunderstand the instructions and get your wires crossed, you will get no shining lights or buzzing buzzers. Even worse—you might get shocked or electrocuted!

Mental health is no different. If you have a sufficient understanding of the Principles of Universal Mind, Consciousness, and Thought and allow the power of Thought to operate in your best interest—your mental health will flourish. On the other hand, if you have an insufficient understanding of the Three Principles and innocently misuse the power of Thought—your mental health will suffer!

The Three Principles don't care if you understand them any more than the Principle behind electricity cares if you understand it. Principles are Principles—facts are facts! If you clearly understand, respect, and align yourself with Principles—things will work quite well. On the other hand, if you don't understand, respect, and allow Principles to work in your favor—innocent or not—things will malfunction. If you fall off a roof, gravity doesn't care—it just pushes you down—splat! If you have an insufficient insight-based understanding of the Three Principles, they won't care either; they will escort you to chronic mental stress.

The Three Principles and Other Psycho-Spiritual Teachings

Jack Pransky and I researched and described the following relationships between The Three Principles and other psychospiritual teachings. For a more in-depth discussion of these relationships, I recommend Jack's book, *Prevention from the Inside-Out*. Universal Mind or similar constructs are evident in all psycho-spiritual teachings. For example,

Sri Arobindo saw Mind as the Power behind Thought and Conscious-ness and asserted that our physical organism no more causes or explains Thought and Consciousness than the construction of an engine explains the motive-power of steam or electricity. The force is anterior, not the physical instrument. Nisargadatta Maharaj asserted that everything is One. Buddhism teaches Master Mind. Vipassana meditation teaches that Mind is everywhere. Denise Hart stated, "The whole body contains the Mind." Neal Donald Walsch pointed to Mind, stating, "That which you call life… is pure energy… vibrating constantly, always… while objects are different and discrete, the energy, which produces them, is exactly the same." William James referred to the "spiritual self" as "Absolute Mind."

Consciousness is also a major component of virtually all psycho-spiritual teachings. For example, Sri Aurobindo stated, "It is conscious-ness that… determines the form or the evolution of form." Siddha Yoga teaches that life is spirit. The Upanishads proposed that prana springs from inner consciousness and moves through the body enlivening its functions. According to the Pratyabhijna Hridayam, "Consciousness is one with the self, so the mind is simply that aspect of the Self which has taken the form of outer objects." A. H. Almaas stated, "The spiritual and the psychological… are two dimensions of the same human conscious-ness." Neville Goddard asserted, "Man moves in a world that is nothing more or less than his consciousness objectified." A Course in Miracles posits that within each individual soul "is the purest of Consciousness." William James related consciousness to thought stating, "The conscious-ness of Self involves a changeable stream of thought… a thought that at each moment, is different from that of the last moment."

Thought is also a prominent teaching in many psycho-spiritual tradi-tions. For example, Vipassana meditation posits that all mental events correspond with sensations in the body. Hart stated, "Thought is pure energy." A Course in Miracles proposes that people have a choice to think that they are either separate or special or connected to God. Unity teaches that people create their psychological lives from within using the power of Thought. Charles Filmore stated, "Every man is king of his own mental domain, and his subjects are his thoughts." Nathaniel Branden described thought as "the power to translate the possibilities of our minds into the reality of our world." William James (1981) connected the "spiritual self" to Thought and stated, "Our considering the spiritual self at all is a reflective process... We can feel, alongside of the thing known, the thought of it going on as an altogether separate act and operation in the mind."

What Sydney Banks uncovered and contributed was the way these spiritual facts of Universal Mind, Consciousness, and Thought work together to create everyone's psychological life. Perhaps some would dispute Banks's notion of how these Principles work together as theory except that they would have to be using these very Principles to dispute it. Jack Pransky concluded, "The point is that no matter what the spiritual teaching ... it always seems to boil down to Mind, Consciousness, and Thought. The trick lies in seeing how they all work together, which is how they can be of most use to us."

The Link Between the Spiritual and the Psychological

It is also helpful to contrast the way the connection between the psychological and the spiritual is viewed from the "inside-out/nothing-missing" paradigm of the Three Principles understanding and the "outside-in/something-missing" paradigm of positive psychology.

Positive Psychology's "Outside-In/Something-Missing" View

Virtues and character strengths which were largely the subject matter of theology, philosophy, and spirituality have become a central framework for positive psychology. For example, wisdom, transcendence, kindness, love, forgiveness, purpose, and meaning-making—core subject matter of most religious and spiritual perspectives—are now a major focus of positive psychology. In this regard, positive psychologists, Christopher Peterson and Martin Seligman, completed what they referred to as, "... the most ambitious project self-consciously undertaken from the perspective of positive psychology." These researchers examined the philosophical, religious, and spiritual traditions of China (Confucianism and Taoism), South Asia (Buddhism and Hinduism), and the West and Ancient Near East (Ancient Greek philosophy, Judaism, Christianity, and Islam). Their goal was to uncover common virtues in these traditions that relate to a pleasant, virtuous, and engaged life.

Subsequently, Peterson and Seligman used the understandings gained from their search to develop positive psychology's counterpart to the DSM-V (psychiatry's diagnostic manual) which they called *Character Strengths and Virtues: A Handbook and Classification (or CSV)*. The CSV describes and classifies six virtues—wisdom, courage, humanity, justice, temperance, and transcendence—that are endorsed by virtually every culture to enable human thriving. Based on positive correlations found between these virtues and mental well-being, Peterson and Seligman concluded that people who are not flourishing are either missing certain virtues or these virtues have eroded over time. Thus, the objective of positive psychology's "psycho-spiritual interventions" is to put certain virtues *into people* via teaching them various techniques (e.g., meditation), beliefs (e.g., the higher purpose and meaning of the universe), and behaviors (e.g., sending a letter of gratitude to someone). Their "outside-in/something-missing" focus is on "interventions that *build* happiness... the *deliberate cultivation* of character strengths... "

The Three Principles' "Inside-Out/Nothing-Missing" View

Sydney Banks viewed Universal Mind, Consciousness, and Thought as spiritual Principles—an inseparable, interrelated trinity that provides a connection between the formless life force and the world of form. Drawing from all possibilities inherent within Universal Mind, people use the power of Thought to create their thoughts. Via people's spiritual power to have consciousness, these thoughts enter people's consciousness and create their personal "realities" and produce feelings based upon the self-created "realities" people see. The spiritual energy behind all life is also Oneness itself, and this pure state manifests in every human being as pure consciousness, which essentially is a state of pure peace, pure love, and pure wisdom. Only one's personal thoughts entering consciousness can create the illusion of separation from this pure state of mental and spiritual health.

The power of Thought creates people's thoughts. The power of Consciousness brings these thoughts alive and allows people to be aware of the forms they create. People can either be "caught" in their thought forms, or they can be the observer of them, or they can see them for what they are—*thought-created illusions*. Each perspective will give people a different experience. People make use of these Principles to create their psychological lives whether they know they are doing this or not. Sydney Banks saw mental health as the innate capacity of all people to align their personal mind with Universal Mind—an innate, intrinsic, natural state arising from pure consciousness—or the capacity of people to realize the infinite capacity for the formless creation of new experiences from within.

A DEEPER DIVE

On YouTube watch:

Sydney Banks – The Truth Lies Within

Sydney Banks on the Three Principles as One Spiritual Psychological Experience

3 Principles: Always True with Annika Hurwitt

PODCAST:

Psychology Has It Backwards, Episode #64—Understanding Principles vs. Theories

CHAPTER 5

Understanding the Power of Thought

Mental health is an innate gift. Everyone has all the mental health they need already inside them. Well-being, wisdom, and resilient functioning exist within the core or essence of everyone. We all can realize and sustain this health because it is our natural state. George Pransky described the transcendent intelligence of this innate health:

> "When we observed the operation of [innate mental health] in ourselves and our clients, we were struck by the intelligence and responsiveness of this [health]. We noticed that this [health] gave people ideas that were clearly beyond the capabilities of their own learning and experience. Children display wisdom beyond their years. People like Albert Einstein come up with theories beyond their education that must be analyzed and proven by people with much more education and expertise than themselves. We've all had the experience of coming up with ideas and thinking to ourselves, 'I'm amazed that I could come up with an idea like that.' Writers and musicians will admit puzzlement about the quality of their creations, admitting that their products are way beyond their education and their known level of expertise. There is obviously a transcendent intelligence behind [this health] that enables us to come up with original ideas and that enables us to have thoughts that are beyond our memories, our experience, and our education."

Using the Power of Thought in Our Best Interest

Every morsel of our psychological lives is created "through us" from the "inside-out" via our thoughts made to appear real via our consciousness. When people have an insufficient understanding of this fact, they tend to relate to their psychological experiences as if they were "the truth"—the way things really are. Also, they tend to believe that their psychological experiences are created by "stuff out there." The unfortunate consequence of this innocent misunderstanding is that—*most people misuse this creative power—chronically obscuring or covering over their innate health—and often experience themselves as the victims of their circumstances.*

We all work much like human movie projectors—consciousness continually projects our thoughts onto our psychological screens. We are never the victims of our circumstances—just the victims of our own insufficient understanding of the Principles and our innocent misuse of the power of Thought. As time passed, we all learned various ways to misuse the power of Thought. Some of us learned to worry—to ruminate—to think in a wandering, ambivalent way—to judge and "fault-find,"—to have a busy, over-active, analytical mind—to construct an ego or self-image (who we *think* we are). Over time, it's likely that you—like me—began spending more and more time innocently misusing the power of Thought—experiencing mental stress and other discomforting feelings—and spending less time fully present in the moment, allowing the power of innate mental health (i.e., Universal Mind) to guide you.

When people lack a sufficient understanding of who they really are—*the Three Principles in action*—their innocent misuse of the power of Thought increases, and their innate mental health gets covered over more often. Over time, people's original view of life as "a smorgasbord of intriguing possibilities" begins to wither. Many of life's possibilities begin to appear "off- limits"—perhaps danger zones to be avoided at all costs. For example, consider the responses of my university students when I asked them the following questions, "How many of you can sing?" (a few hands slowly go up); "How many of you can dance?" (a few more hands go up); How many of you can act?" (fewer hands are raised). Then, I asked them this one, "What response would I get if I asked these same questions to a Kindergarten class?" They all get it—every little hand would be on deck!" *The only thing that can obscure our innate mental health is our own insufficient understanding and misuse of the power of Thought.*

Personal Thought

Personal (or analytical thought) is essential for many purposes such as logistics, financial calculations, and comparisons—anything that requires applying a known formula to some known variables. For example, when one calculates the amount of fabric to make a dress—figures out the logistics for a wedding reception—decides when to leave for the airport to catch a flight—they recall (or look up) the necessary thoughts and hold them in mind until they accomplish their task.

Many skills and habits people pick up using personal thought are very useful. Basic skills like reading, writing, and math—complex skills like driving a car, hitting a golf ball, repairing an engine, and doing brain surgery (at least at first) require personal thought. Eventually, skills mastered via personal thought can be taken over and carried out more effortlessly via Universal Mind. For example, you likely don't have to figure out how to drive to work every day. You simply get in your vehicle—start the engine—and allow Universal Mind to guide you.

Mental health—with its effortless flow of intelligent thoughts—is an innate gift. Personal thought, however, has to be learned and practiced. Innate health is effortless. Personal thought, on the other hand, promotes *a stress factor* because holding thoughts in mind and entertaining, manipulating, ruminating on, or working with them *takes effort.* That's why young children often resist learning skills that require personal thinking. It can be difficult at first to get a young child to sit still—attend to certain thoughts—hold them in mind—to master essential skills like counting, reading, telling time, and tying shoelaces.

Overusing Personal Thought

The effort of personal thought can generate chronic mental stress. In other words, personal thinking is subject to *overuse*. Even when used for purposes it is designed for, such as doing taxes or studying for exams, overusing personal thought (e.g., exam cramming) can generate chronic mental stress—even burnout! George Pransky put it this way:

> "Even if it is used properly, people who do too much personal thinking experience fatigue, exaggerated mood swings, and excessive emotionality. To overuse personal thought would be equivalent to abusing the body with sleep deprivation and expending energy beyond a person's own tolerances. People who have overactive minds through excessive use of personal thought experience boredom and stress."

I used to do hour after hour of psychotherapy with personal thought at the helm. I seldom trusted my innate health (Universal Mind) to guide my sessions. Heck, I didn't even know then that innate health existed! My therapy sessions were typically stressful—often draining—for me and my clients. Overusing personal thinking to "analyze" my clients' pasts, feelings, and behaviors and search with them for solutions for their "issues" and "problems" was typical for most therapists then and still is today for many. That's a major reason why "burnout" in our profession is so common. Before I gained a sufficient understanding of the Three Principles, I thought my stress came from "doing therapy." Now, I realize that *a major source of my stress was overusing personal thought.*

Even dwelling on an exciting thought can compromise one's mental health. Consider a teenage boy who "can't stop thinking" about a cute girl at school. Day and night he thinks about her. He can't get her out of his mind. Engulfed in these "exciting" thoughts—he avoids his homework, ignores his friends, and skips meals. What some might call "puppy love" is actually a case of the "mental flu" caused by overusing personal thought.

Today, most everyone realizes that smoking can prevent their lungs from breathing efficiently and that bad cholesterol can prevent their blood from flowing freely through their arteries. However, most people don't realize that when any thought is held in mind too long—even for a worthwhile purpose—one's mental health can suffer like one's physical health can suffer when unhealthy physical habits interfere with the natural operation of their body.

Misusing Personal Thought

Personal thought is also subject to misuse. For example, if one or both of your parents habitually entertained angry thoughts, you may have picked up a "bad temper." If one or both parents were continually analyzing—compulsively planning— always "spinning their wheels"—you may have developed a busy, overly-active, analytical mind. If a parent worried chronically or habitually judged and found fault with just about everything, you may have learned to be a "worrier" and/or a "fault-finder." Three Principles educator, Allan Flood, describes how he acquired the habit of "worrying" from his mother:

> "My mother is the quintessential worrier. When I told her yesterday I was finding time to study for an exam while I was walking the dog, her immediate response was to warn me to be careful and not trip and hurt myself. So, when growing up, I learned the tendency to "squeeze" thoughts of potential danger by worrying about them - holding them in my mind longer than necessary. Understanding the three Principles gives me the perspective to disrespect these thoughts and not squeeze them as hard—to have faith in my natural thinking [innate health] to look for the potholes."

There is a personal thought "overuse and misuse" pandemic going on out there. Most people horribly overuse and misuse personal thought. In fact, personal thought is what most people (and most mainstream psychologists) view as "normal" thinking—perhaps the only way that people are able to use the power of Thought. *For most people—and most mainstream psychologists—personal thought has become the master of their psychological lives!*

Thought Reconditioning Is Not the Answer

Some of you may be wondering, "Okay—I realize that my psychological life is being created "through me" from the "inside-out" via my use of the Three Principles—*particularly my use of the power of Thought.* However, I'm still not sure how to take up residence in the land of flourishing mental health. Should I challenge and refute my discomforting personal thoughts? Should I try to think more positive thoughts? Should I search for ways to distract myself from my negative personal thoughts? Should I meditate—use positive affirmations—how about self-hypnosis?"

Most people think that the way to a flourishing mental life is to work hard at challenging and reconditioning their personal thoughts and beliefs, persistently practice various mind-quieting techniques, and find ways to distract themselves from, or to suppress, their discomforting thoughts. Scads of mainstream psychologists support these methods and techniques. I used to encourage my therapy clients to challenge and recondition their discomforting thoughts and fight their irrational beliefs. I didn't realize then that these thought-reconditioning techniques required loads of additional personal thinking which resulted in added stress for many clients—didn't help them realize the "inside-out" creation of people's psychological lives—didn't assist them to "see" that they have all the mental health they need already inside them.

The truth is—you don't have to do a lick of thought reconditioning, deliberate mind-quieting activities, or distraction techniques to realize and sustain mental well-being. You don't have to uncover and refute any discomforting thoughts or irrational beliefs. You don't have to practice positive thinking, guided imagery, or positive affirmations! The compulsive use of such tools and techniques is merely another version of the "more/better/different" game that we visited earlier—I'll be happier if I work hard at thinking *more* positive thoughts—get *better* at challenging my negative thoughts—try to think about my circumstances in a *different* way.

The Optimal Use of the Power of Thought

Innate health (i.e., Universal Mind)—not personal thought—is meant to be the master or director of our psychological lives. When we realize the incredible power of this health and trust it to guide us, it will signal us—provide us with an intelligent thought—to use personal thought when personal thinking makes sense in the moment. In sum, *personal thought is meant to be the faithful servant of Universal Mind.*

In a nutshell, *the optimal use of the creative power of Thought involves a balanced movement, back and forth, between a spontaneous reliance on the intelligence of Universal Mind (i.e., innate mental health) and the use of personal thought when prompted by this innate intelligence.* In other words, the primary characteristic of people who generally live in mental well-being is the responsive balance of innate health (an effortless flow of intelligent thoughts) and personal thought in their everyday lives.

While writing this book, I typically trusted Universal Mind to guide me. Often, fresh thoughts "popped" into my head. Helpful words and examples came to mind seemingly out of the blue. Occasionally, a useful thought would surface faster than I could write it down. At times, old memories came to mind in fresh, creative ways. I didn't try to retrieve them—they just showed up. Hours passed and often it seemed like minutes! If a less useful thought appeared, innate health would prompt me to "let it float by." Often, I felt like a receiver or channel through which some Higher Power was guiding me—and it was!

Occasionally, Universal Mind would nudge me to "bone up" on a particular topic. Then, I would switch to personal thinking and perhaps do some research. While personal thinking took effort—it was helpful and appropriate. After using personal thought for a while, I would notice some stressful feelings—another signal from Universal Mind to allow my personal mind to quiet down.

Unfortunately, most people horribly underuse the state of innate health and grossly overuse and misuse personal thought. The overuse and misuse of personal thought and the chronic mental stress it spawns are the primary factors in the etiology, persistence, co-occurrence, and sequential comorbidity of myriad psychological disorders. Unfortunately, most people don't often realize that they are creating their own psychological discomfort—and often physical ill-health—via chronically misusing personal thinking. George Pransky put it this way:

"As people learn, in essence, to leave their thinking alone—that is, to let [Universal Mind] guide them in and out of [personal] thought as needed and to refrain from grabbing onto any thought and deliberately thinking it, their thinking is increasingly fruitful, productive, wise, and common-sense…"

In sum, human psychological functioning is the same as human physiological functioning *in that both are self-correcting*. Innate mental health is the state to which people's minds return readily and naturally when they cease hanging onto and ruminating over the content of their personal thinking—in the same way that "natural" breathing engages when a sprinter out of breath stops running.

A DEEPER DIVE

Watch on YOUTUBE:

Sydney Banks: Our True Identity

Innate Health: Eliminating Stress and Creating a Healthy Community #1

A Psychiatrist's Perspective on Innate Health: Bill Pettit

Alter Your Health #60: Dicken Bettinger: From Stress and Chaos to Peace and Wisdom

The Space Within with Michael Neil—A Wholeness Hangout

CHAPTER 6

Only One Mental Illness

Bill Pettit, Judy Sedgeman, Jack Pransky, and I co-authored a paper that describes the Three Principles' "inside-out/nothing-missing" view of the common liability in all forms of mental ill-health. Mainstream psychology typically refers to this common liability as "general factor p." Our paper was published in the *Journal of Spiritual Psychology and Counseling* (Kelley, Pettit, Sedgeman, & Pransky, 2021). A summary of our Three Principles-based view of general factor p follows.

General Factor p

For several decades, Sydney Banks and several other Three Principles pioneers, practitioners, and researchers asserted—*there is only one generic mental illness!* Recently, mainstream psychology has also noticed that a common factor or liability appears to underly a variety of mental illness diagnoses. For example, mainstream psychologists, Avshalom Caspi and Terri Moffit, stated:

> "…empirical evidence has accrued to suggest that a single dimension is able to measure a person's liability to mental disorder, comorbidity among disorders, persistence of disorders over time, and severity of symptoms."

Research regarding internalizing (e.g., depression, anxiety), externalizing (e.g., conduct disorder), and psychotic symptoms (e.g., hallucinations, delusions) across the life span also point to a general factor of psychopathology commonly referred to by mainstream psychology as *general factor p*. Considerable evidence from genetic, neuroscience, and risk-factor research also points to a shared cause underlying an array of mental disorders.

The "p factor" appears to capture the shared variance across psychiatric symptoms, predict a multitude of poor outcomes and general life impairment, and account for the co-occurrence of internalizing disorders and externalizing disorders. This unidimensional factor reflects a model of psychopathology in which symptoms wax and wane, and individuals cycle through different psychiatric diagnoses over time *because they have a general vulnerability to psychopathology rather than any specific disorder.*

While mainstream psychology has yet to identify this p factor, it has offered several speculations including *negative emotionality, cognitive impulsivity, a deficiency in intellectual functioning, and symptoms of disordered thought processes.* However, rather than illuminating p, these kinds of speculations reflect mainstream psychology's misdirected "outside-in/something-missing" paradigm. In other words, these speculations shine light on some of the myriad negative or unhealthy manifestations of this common liability.

To understand what p is requires a shift in focus away from the negative effects of p to the very source of these ill-effects. Multiple forms of psychopathology can be viewed from the same basis because they are all created in the same way—*via people's insufficient understanding of the Three Principles and innocent misuse of the power of Thought.* In other words, the common liability regarding all forms of psychopathology (i.e., general factor p) is *an insufficient understanding, via insight, of the way the Principles of Universal Mind, Consciousness, and Thought manifest within everyone to create their psychological life experiences.* A path from the Three Principles' view of general factor p to psychopathology and its symptoms follows.

A Path from General Factor p to Psychopathology

An Insufficient Insight-Based Understanding of the Three Principles (i.e., p)

Whether people realize it or not, *the Principles of Universal Mind, Consciousness, and Thought are constantly creating their psychological lives from the "inside-out."* Regarding any system (e.g., biological, chemical, mechanical), with a sufficient understanding of the system's undergirding Principles, people can use the Principles in their best interest. On the other hand, if the system's Principles are insufficiently understood, people can innocently misuse them and hurt themselves. Whether people typically use the Three Principles in their favor or to the detriment of their well-being, wisdom and resilient functioning stems from their level of insight-based understanding of the way these Principles manifest within everyone to create their psychological lives.

Innocent Misuse of the Power of Thought

Universal Mind continually powers Thought and Consciousness to create everyone's psychological life. Consciousness continually converts whatever thoughts it encounters into people's experienced realities. The only variable in this Principle-based understanding of p is the Principle of Thought. "That people think" is not a variable because everyone is constantly thinking. People do have a say, however, regarding what thoughts they hold in mind, the meaning they attribute to their thoughts with other thoughts, and how they relate to the products of their thoughts (e.g., feelings, states of mind, symptoms). Absent a sufficient insight-based understanding of the Three Principles, people are prone to innocently misuse the power of Thought and to believe and act on the ideas, perceptions, and feelings their biased, personal thoughts create.

In this regard, the consensus of voluminous psychopathology research is that maladaptive, repetitive personal thought is a common factor in numerous forms of psychopathology. For example, psychologist Bart Verkuil stated:

> "… in psychopathology research, perseverative cognitive processes (i.e., stress-producing cognitions that are repeatedly activated) like worry and rumination have received increasing attention… and have been recognized as core etiological factors in the onset and maintenance of several psychological disorders."

The chronic misuse of the power of Thought relates positively with depressed mood and pessimism, clinical depression, heightened anger, posttraumatic stress disorder or PTSD symptomology, increased anxiety, difficulty concentrating, poor problem-solving, poor sleep quality, reduced quality of life, worse physical health, worse cardiovascular function, and weakened immune system function. These findings are supported by several meta-analyses (i.e., examination of data from several independent studies of the same subject, to determine overall trends) demonstrating the negative effects of the chronic misuse of the power of Thought across a wide range of psychological and somatic ill-health.

Furthermore, misuse of the power of Thought to control one's discomforting personal thoughts following their creation (e.g., suppression, cognitive self-consciousness, self-beratement, thought reconditioning) has also been identified as an important feature of numerous psychological disorders such as obsessive-compulsive disorder, PTSD, hypochondriasis, social phobia, insomnia, and depression. Additional research suggests that unconscious perseverative thought also plays a role in creating and sustaining many psychological and somatic disorders. Sydney Banks stated, "Mental health lies within the consciousness of all human beings, but it is shrouded and held prisoner by our own erroneous thoughts."

Chronic Mental Stress

Chronic misuse of the power of Thought and the discomforting experiences it spawns regarding the past (e.g., guilt, resentment, unresolved grief), the present (e.g., self-consciousness, ego, agitation), and the future (e.g., apprehension, fear, terror) typically results in chronic mental stress. It is important to distinguish chronic mental stress—the long-term, on-going experience of mental stress—from acute or temporary mental stress that prepares the mind and body to respond to challenging life circumstances and are followed by a return to homeostasis or balance when a challenge passes. The human body is designed to occasionally experience acute stress and recover. Acute stress is part of the regular cycle of life and does no harm. A state of chronic mental stress, however, keeps the body in a constant state of psychological and somatic arousal or alarm. Psychologist, Robert Sapolsky, described it this way:

> "If you repeatedly turn on the stress response, or if you cannot turn off the stress response… the stress response can eventually become damaging. A large percentage of what we think of when we talk about stress-related diseases are disorders of excessive stress-responses."

In sum, chronic mental stress can negatively impact the entire human experience—psychologically, physiologically, and spiritually.

Another consensus of voluminous psychopathology research is that multiple forms of mental ill-health, often with concomitant physiological consequences, are initiated and perpetuated by chronic activation of the stress response system. Chronic mental stress typically results in overproduction of cortisol, noradrenaline, and other stress hormones, heightened inflammation, changes in the reactivity of the hypothalamic-pituitary-adrenal axis, and disturbances in homeostasis in the neurotransmitters and receptors and the brain's neuro-circuitry. Overexposure to stress hormones can disrupt the immune system and the microbiota, the digestive system, the reproductive system, and the growth processes. This complex, natural alarm system also communicates with regions of the brain that control mood, motivation, and fear, potentially creating a variety of negative and often debilitating psychological symptoms.

These dysregulations can also produce multiple somatic changes, including lowered pain tolerance, sleep disturbance, muscle tension, and autoimmune dysregulation that add to the psychological burden. In sum, Brosschot, Verkuil, and Theyer stated:

> "… humans, have a unique ability to make cognitive representations of events from the past and from the anticipated future. The downside is that we are able to ruminate about the past and worry about the future… It is this ability that seems to make chronic stress a recent 'invention' of mankind… Our ability to worry… enables us to extend our stress experiences nearly endlessly in both directions, past and future…"

Psychopathology

If the psychological and somatic symptoms of chronic mental stress progress with sufficient severity and persistence, and treatment is sought, they are categorized as common psychiatric disorders such as major depression, generalized anxiety, and social phobia. At severe levels, they are classified as psychotic experiences and diagnoses. A path from the Three Principles-based view of general factor p to psychopathology/obscured mental health is illustrated in Figure 1.

Figure 1: A Path from the Three Principles-Based View of General Factor p to Psychopathology/Obscured Mental Health

Insufficient Understanding, via Insight, of the Three Principles (i.e., General Factor p)

↓

Innocent Misuse of the Power of Thought

↓

Chronic Mental Stress

↙   ↘

Psychopathology   **Obscured Innate Mental Health**

Discomforting Symptoms Are "Our Friends"

Viewed through the logic of the Three Principles understanding, mainstream psychology's prevailing speculations regarding the identity of general factor p (i.e., negative emotionality, poor emotional control, impulsive behavior, vulnerability to psychopathology, symptoms of disordered thought processes) do not illuminate p. Rather, these speculations shed light on a few of the myriad discomforting manifestations of p. *More importantly, these ill-effects are natural products of the Three Principles in action. In other words, emotional instability, impulsivity, poor emotional control, vulnerability to psychopathology, and symptoms of disordered thought processes are internal alarms attempting to alert people that they are misusing the power of Thought and innocently obscuring their innate mental health!*

Mainstream Psychology's "Outside-In" View of Stress

Mainstream psychology's prevailing view is that stress is a "real" and unremitting factor, a condition for which people must find an appropriate response, and that stressful thoughts must be "dealt with" for people to recover. For example, neuroscientist, George Stefano, defined stress as follows:

> "Today, stress is a generic term that is defined as the effects of psychosocial and environmental factors on physical or mental well-being. We live in a modern world with fast-paced technological advancements, strengthening forces of globalization, and swelling amounts of information to digest. As we become busier and are bombarded by more stimuli each day, we find ourselves in increasingly stressful situations."

In contrast, Three Principles psychiatrist, Bill Pettit, defined stress as a "… physiological, psychological, spiritual experience of the 'dance' of negative/insecure thoughts through our limbic system and senses." Via a sufficient understanding of the Three Principles, one recognizes that stress is created from the "inside-out"—a byproduct of the dynamic process of thought brought to life by consciousness. Three Principles mental health educator, Judy Sedgeman, stated:

> "Since all thoughts are ephemeral and illusory, stressful thinking, like any other thinking, will pass more readily if the thinker understands how thought works. With that understanding, people come to see the feeling state of stress, (i.e., a stressful state of mind) as a warning signal to leave upsetting thinking alone, rather than ruminating on it. [With this understanding] they naturally return to a positive feeling state and [heathier] thinking [and] regain access to clarity and common sense, the wellsprings of their ability to respond constructively and creatively to life events."

A DEEPER DIVE

On YouTube watch:

Sydney Banks – The Answers Lie Within You

There is Only One Mental Illness with Bill Pettit

The Profound Simplicity of Mental Health with Mark Howard

Never Broken Never Lacking with Bill Pettit

Book:

Somebody Should Have Told Us! by Jack Pransky

CHAPTER 7

A Path from Three Principles Exposure to Improved Mental Health

Jack Pransky, Eric Lambert, and I co-authored a paper that describes a path from exposure to the Principles of Universal Mind, Consciousness, and Thought to improved mental health/improved behavior. Our paper was published in the American Psychological Association sponsored journal, *Spirituality in Clinical Practice* (Kelley, Pransky, & Lambert, 2015). A summary of this path follows.

Three Principles Exposure

To varying degrees, most people attribute the source of their psychological experiences to external events and circumstances. Also, most people tend to believe that their perceptions are "reality," and that they must act on the "realities" they see. With exposure to the Three Principles, however, people have an opportunity to recognize that their psychological lives are created from the "inside-out" via their own thoughts—no matter what occurs "out there,"—and that while the "realities" they experience appear to be "the truth," they are, in fact, *temporary thought plus consciousness illusions.*

Three Principles Understanding

Because people are exposed to the Three Principles does not ensure they will grasp sufficient insight regarding the way the Principles manifest within everyone. By understanding, we mean sufficient insight regarding the way the Principles work in every person to create their experienced realities. Not only an intellectual understanding, but "seeing" the Principles in operation in their own and others' lives. Without a sufficient *insight-based* understanding, exposure to the Principles would likely have little or no effect on people's mental health and behavior. However, while a sufficient understanding of the Three Principles is essential, it is not sufficient for people to realize and sustain improved mental health and behavior. People who understand the Three Principles must also experience a sufficient insight-based understanding of at least one of the following—*the power of Thought and the power of innate mental health.*

The Power of Thought

Sufficient recognition of the power of Thought means that people realize that Thought, in interaction with Consciousness, is the only reality people can ever know and is the source of everyone's perceptions, feelings, and states of mind. People who grasp a sufficient understanding of the power of Thought "see" that what looks real is one's own inadvertent creation—a momentary illusion enlivened by consciousness. People with sufficient understanding of the power of Thought also recognize that their thinking creates a changed "reality" with each new thought and yields resultant feelings, perceptions, and states of mind—or they recognize it later as a self-correcting function. This understanding improves the way people use the power of Thought and how they relate to the products of their thinking (e.g., thoughts, beliefs, feelings, perceptions, states of mind, symptoms). With a sufficient understanding, people can look before thought content or "what they think" to the way their thoughts are created and then experienced (i.e., the Power to think).

People can have varying degrees of this understanding. When this awareness/realization is insufficient, people have less perspective regarding the way their psychological experiences are created. With sufficient awareness/realization, people have a greater ability to be resilient and unaffected by their personal thinking. They see the thought-experience connection more clearly. Consequently, they adjust to discomforting moods and life challenges more easily and are typically resilient during challenge and flux. They see their experience of life—their reality—as subjective because it is based on their own thinking, making them humbler and more open-minded about the validity of any thought; they see their beliefs as opinions rather than absolute truths. They are less likely to overuse and misuse personal thought and spend more of their waking moments allowing their innate health/wisdom (i.e., Universal Mind) to guide them. Therefore, their typical feeling state is one of well-being. George Pransky put it this way:

> "The principles of Mind, Consciousness, and Thought provide understanding that makes healthy functioning and well-being a psychological way of life rather than a chance occurrence. People's level of understanding provides a permanent foundation for their well-being. Once people realize as a personal insight and not just an intellectual concept, the link between thought and well-being, they will naturally gravitate toward… healthy functioning. The realization of the link between thought and well-being is specifically the understanding of their psychological lives… When a level of well-being is supported by a corresponding jump in level of understanding [of the power of Thought and/or the power of innate mental health] only then will the level of well-being be permanent."

The Power of Innate Mental Health

The second major realm of insight-based understanding is that everyone has all the mental health they need already inside them—that the only thing that can obscure this health is one's discomforting personal thoughts taken to heart in the moment—and that everyone has direct access to this health via realizing its power and trusting it to guide them. Three Principles psychologist, Elana Mustakova-Possardt, stated:

> "Mental health is the innate capacity of every person to return into alignment with [Universal] Mind… and manifest fresh understanding and creative responsiveness in the moment… [and] the experience of peace, contentment, larger perspective on immediate reality, detachment and a generous, loving, and deeply moral view of life."

This "inside-out/nothing-missing" paradigm views mental well-being as the natural default setting for all people. It posits that human psychological functioning is the same as human physiological functioning *in that both are self-correcting*. Innate mental health is the state to which people's minds return readily and naturally when they cease hanging onto and ruminating over the content of their personal thinking in the same way that "natural" breathing engages when a runner out of breath stops running.

In sum, for insights in both realms to make a difference for improved mental health, they need to be seen in action in one's own life and generalized to all other lives. It would appear possible for people to have only one of these insights and still have improved mental health, but either of these insights can occur at different levels. The deeper the level, the greater the positive change expected in one's mental health and behavior.

When a person recognizes that a thought is just a thought and/or realizes the profound resource of innate well-being/wisdom/resilient functioning, they see the foolishness of obscuring their innate health via misusing the power of Thought (e.g., to worry, ruminate, over-analyze, etc.). Judy Sedgeman stated:

> "From the vantage point of … a positive feeling, people are able to address even the most daunting life circumstances with insight

and common sense and find creative solutions to life challenges. People are able to see the content of their thinking as variable and recognize that things that appear unmanageable or insoluble in one state of mind appear manageable and soluble in another, even if the circumstances have not changed."

Elsie Spittle added:

"We are always thinking, but there is a different quality of thought when we are not erecting barriers to our innate wisdom. Insightful thoughts fill the space left by all the negative, worrisome thoughts we used to entertain so much. These new thoughts are calming, inspiring, exhilarating, and exceedingly helpful. These thoughts guide us to a better life."

As people's understanding of the power of Thought deepens, they spend less time misusing this creative power and obscuring their innate health. In turn, their mental stress, and the symptoms of mental (and physical) ill-health it spawns (e.g., anxiety, depression, anger) lessen. Sydney Banks explains:

"Let your negative thoughts go. They are nothing more than passing thoughts. You are then on your way to finding the peace of mind you seek, having healthier feelings for yourself and for others. This is simple logic."

Improved Mental Health/Improved Behavior

When people gain a sufficient understanding of the Three Principles, and, in turn, grasp sufficient insight regarding the power of Thought and/or the power of innate mental health, they will experience improved mental health. Although there are many definitions of mental health, all appear to have *"well-being"* in common. Furthermore, everyone behaves in synch with the way their thoughts make their lives appear to them.

Thus, improved mental health is typically accompanied by more responsive behaviors. Roger Mills stated:

> "When people recognize how the Three Principles work, they gain tremendous freedom and clarity… the ability to live life at its highest potential. As people begin to see how reality is created, moment-by-moment, through the interweaving of these Principles, they realize their innate creative power and resilience, their own wisdom and beauty, and their genuine potential for a gratifying life."

In sum, the common underpinning for all work in this "inside-out/nothing-missing" paradigm is bringing people to their own insight-based understanding of the Three Principles—*Universal Mind, the formless energy and intelligence behind all life*—*Consciousness, the power to be aware of life and experience thought as reality*—*Thought, the power to create forms or ideas from that formless energy.* Judy Sedgeman summed it up this way:

> "The Three Principles point towards a different paradigm: the realization that the ability to form thought and experience one's changing thinking as reality is the only factor that creates all the infinite expressions of thoughts, feelings, and behavior. An external circumstance "unthought" is not experienced; external events do not form thought, but rather thoughts in formation create our perceptions and experience of external events, moment-to-moment. This Principle-based paradigm did not evolve from what has gone before. This paradigm represents a revolution in the way the mental health and prevention fields view human nature and human behavior and promote change. The assumptions of the prevailing "outside-in" paradigm are quite clear. The assumptions of this inside-out paradigm are completely different."

A DEEPER DIVE

Jack Pransky and I co-authored a paper that proposed a scientific basis for how the formless comes into form. In this paper, we offer evidence for a scientific justification of the Principles of Universal Mind, Consciousness, and Thought. Our paper was published in *Cogent Psychology* (Pransky& Kelley, 2017). A summary follows.

Thought: The Fundamental Property Of Human Experience

Edward O. Wilson emphasized that what humans call "reality" is an empirical question that can be answered only by probing the physical basis of the thought process. Wilson proposed that thought makes something happen—that thought is part of some process that results in physical form. David Bohm, a student of Albert Einstein, emphasized that thought does not tell people that it is participating in and altering the very way things are. According to Bohm, "Thought produces something and then says, 'I didn't do it. It's really there." James Jeans posited that the world is more like a thought system than material reality—that people perceive only illusions of the real world. Bohm saw the universe as a unified network of events and relationships in which the mind and human soul are integral parts of existence, rather than merely products of nature. He emphasized that many physicists believe this is a fundamental event beyond physics—an act of consciousness and thought.

Einstein proved that matter is another form of energy. At the quantum level, there appears to be no real separation between matter and energy. Deepak Chopra stated, "… if you zero in on … bits of subatomic matter, they are not material at all but rather mere vibrations of energy that have taken on the appearance of solidity…" Electrons under the same condition act as particles and then at other times act as waves depending on what the observer expects will happen. At the quantum level, the role of the observer is prominent in determining the nature of reality. What the observer thinks will occur is what the quantum field does. A Principle of quantum physics is "thought determines reality."

Gary Zukav asserted that at each moment people are informing the energy that flows through them with each thought and, since no form exists without consciousness, there is only energy shaped by consciousness. Thought and consciousness appear to be inexorably intertwined. Without consciousness, people would have no experience of their thinking. Sir John Eccles asserted that while evolution can account for the brain, only something transcendent (i.e., Universal Mind) can explain consciousness and thought.

Sydney Banks asserted that Universal Mind, Consciousness, and Thought are the elements through which people create and have experience and that absent any one of the three, people would have no experience—that all psychological experience is propelled by its most fundamental property—Thought. Thought is inextricably linked to and brought to life by Consciousness and powered up by Universal Mind—that "reality" is not what it seems, precisely because thought enters perception and alters whatever people perceive—that consciousness would forever remain a mystery were it not for its connection to thought.

Thought Beyond the Personal Mind

Banks pointed people to a realm beyond the personal mind from which insights, intuition, wisdom, realizations, and revelations spring. While these are also within the domain of thought, they appear to be from a different realm. Bohm corroborated this when asserting insight or intelligence exist beyond people's conditioned thought patterns. Chopra agreed, stating:

> "[Beyond the constant activity of the personal mind] … lies a silent region that appears as empty as the quantum field between the stars. Yet, like the quantum field, our inner silence holds rich promise. The silence inside us is the key to the quantum

mechanical body. It is not chaotic but an organized silence. It has shape and design, purpose, and processes, just like the physical body…"

When people grasp sufficient insight regarding the power of Thought, they can see past their discomforting thoughts and experience higher levels of consciousness where new insights are available that can move the entire process to a healthier place. Sydney Banks stated:

> "As our consciousness ascends, we regain purity of thought, and regain our feelings of love and understanding. Mental health lies within the consciousness of all human beings. This is why we must look past our contaminated thoughts to find the purity and wisdom that lies inside our own consciousness."

Thought and Physical Well-Being

Caroline Myss asserted that because Divine energy is inherent in our biological system, every thought entering our mind, every belief nurtured, and every memory hung onto translates into a positive or negative command to our bodies and spirits. Thus, people may be creating their own physical health via their use of the creative power of Thought. For example, if people have a negative attitude, they may be bombarding their cells with those specific neurotransmitters which, in turn, may be programing their cells to receive more of those neurotransmitters in the future. Worse, those people may be reducing the number of receptors of positive-attitude neurotransmitters, making themselves inclined toward negativity.

Simultaneously, people may inadvertently be creating neural pathways in their brains which more easily allow negative thoughts to travel these pathways like wheels in a rut. Research on neuroplasty appears to support this view. It appears that what people attend to—consciously or unconsciously—results in neurons firing together and wiring together.

For example, George Stefano and associates observed almost immediate changes in nitric oxide (NO), a critical component of the immune system, in response to increasing and decreasing stressful thoughts. The changes in NO were so rapid the researchers speculated they, "… may really represent the manifestation of a proactive mind-body link that evokes an innate protective response."

Jan Kiecolt-Glaser and her associates concluded that negative affect, a characteristic of much of the psychopathology spectrum, is a key pathway for other psychological modifiers of immune function. Conversely, Rollin McCraty posited that through fostering positive emotions and psychophysiological coherence, people can replace habitual, emotional patterns underlying stress with new, healthier patterns that foster increased emotional stability, mental acuity, and physiological efficiency as a new norm. Sydney Banks asserted that it isn't necessary to go out of one's way to reframe one's thoughts or to think more positively because when one ceases to think in a negative manner, healthier thoughts naturally unfold.

The science of epigenetics posits that thought influences the expression of genes. According to Bruce Lipton, genes do not make decisions about being turned on and off. Rather, genes can be considered blueprints that provide potentials, and the human body is structured to develop and regenerate itself from gene blueprints. Lipton viewed thought as the building contractor that adjusts DNA blueprints. Thus, people may be creating their own biology with their use of the power of Thought.

Ilya Prigogine asserted that a closed system will decay and deteriorate. According to Caroline Myss, transmitting energy to the past by dwelling on painful memories draws power from people's bodies and can lead to illness. Dorthe Kirkegaard Thomsen and her associates demonstrated that chronically re-thinking painful memories is associated with physical pain and immune system dysfunction. However, if energy is introduced into the system, the disintegration process is altered, and matter takes on a higher organization. The new energy surfaces spontaneously and the system gets rejuvenated when people realize the "inside-out" creation of everyone's psychological life via use of the Three Principles

A DEEPER DIVE

On YouTube watch:

David Bohm: Thought Has Produced Our Problems

Your Thoughts Create Your Reality: Deepak Chopra

The Power of Intuition and How to Use It: Gary Zukav

How Does One Go to the Very Source of Thought? Jiddu Krishnamurti

PART IV

Understanding The Three Principles

CHAPTER 8

Gauging Your Insight-Based Understanding of the Three Principles

What is your current level of insight-based understanding of the way the Three Principles manifest within everyone to create their psychological life experiences? Do you typically use the power of Thought in your favor? Do you have a sufficient insight-based understanding of the power of innate mental health? The items that follow are designed to assist you to gauge your present level of insight-based understanding of the Three Principles, the power of Thought, and the power of innate mental health—your general level of mental stress and other discomforting experiences, and your typical level of mental well-being. Please don't get serious now... it's just a game!

Step 1: Insight-Based Understanding of The Three Principles, the Power of Thought, and The Power of Innate Mental Health

Directions: For each statement below please circle the number that best represents your answer or position on the statement. *Please answer from your **intuition** (what you know in your heart is true) rather than from your **intellect** (what you think is the right answer).*

ITEMS	Disagree Completely-No Exceptions	Disagree Strongly	Disagree Somewhat	Agree Somewhat	Agree Strongly	Agree Completely-No Exceptions
1. No matter what my circumstances, wisdom is always available to me.	1	2	3	4	5	6
2. Techniques such as positive thinking and meditation are necessary for people to maintain good mental health.	6	5	4	3	2	1
3. The only feelings people can have are created by their thoughts.	1	2	3	4	5	6
4. Sometimes people's moods have nothing to do with their thoughts.	6	5	4	3	2	1
5. If something traumatic happens to someone, it can permanently damage their mental health.	6	5	4	3	2	1
6. When people are angry, they should take it seriously and express it in a healthy way.	6	5	4	3	2	1
7. People's self-esteem can be permanently damaged because of people criticizing them or "putting them down".	6	5	4	3	2	1
8. The only way people can experience stress is because of their thoughts.	1	2	3	4	5	6

ITEMS	Disagree Com-pletely-No Exceptions	Disagree Strongly	Disagree Somewhat	Agree Somewhat	Agree Strongly	Agree Completely-No Exceptions
9. People's thoughts matter more to their well-being than whether they take their thoughts seriously.	1	2	3	4	5	6
10. Everyone is always doing the best they can in the moment.	1	2	3	4	5	6
11. When people are stressed, their stress is usually caused by the situation they are in.	6	5	4	3	2	1
12. Certain past events such as traumatic childhood experiences can make peace of mind impossible.	6	5	4	3	2	1
13. Having more money would make me happier.	6	5	4	3	2	1
14. People's feelings are determined mainly by their situations, circumstances, and how other people treat them.	6	5	4	3	2	1
15. Every experience people have is created by their thinking.	1	2	3	4	5	6

SCORING

Understanding of the Power of Thought—Items 3, 4, 6, 8, 9, 10, 11, 14, & 15

Highest Possible Score = 54   Your Score _____

Understanding the Power of Innate Mental Health—Items 1, 2, 5, 7, 12, & 13

Highest Possible Score = 36   Your Score _____

Step 2: Use of the Power of Thought
(4 parts/12-items)

Part 1-Directions: For each of the following statements, please indicate your level of agreement or disagreement: 1) Strongly Disagree 2) Disagree 3) Neutral 4) Agree 5) Strongly Agree

1. I always seem to be "re-hashing" in my mind recent things I've said or done. 1 2 3 4 5
2. I tend to "ruminate" or dwell over things that happen to me for a really long time afterward. 1 2 3 4 5
3. I spend a great deal of time thinking back over my embarrassing or disappointing moments. 1 2 3 4 5

Part 2-Directions: Please rate each of the following statements on a scale from 1 (not at all typical of me) to 5 (very typical of me).

4. Many situations make me worry. 1 2 3 4 5
5. I am always worrying about something. 1 2 3 4 5
6. Once I start worrying, I cannot stop. 1 2 3 4 5

Part 3-Directions: People think and do many different things when they feel depressed. Please read each of the items below and indicate what you generally do when you feel depressed, *not what you think you should do,* using this scale: 1) Almost Never   2) Sometimes   3) Often   4) Almost Always

7. Analyze recent events to try to understand why you are depressed. 1 2 3 4

8. Think about all your shortcomings, failings, faults, and mistakes. 1 2 3 4

9. Analyze your personality to try to understand why you are depressed. 1 2 3 4

Part 4-Directions: Please indicate how often the following statements apply to you on this scale: 1) almost never 2) sometimes 3) about half the time 4) most of the time 5) almost always

10. When I am upset, I believe that I will remain that way for a long time. 1 2 3 4 5

11. When I am upset, I feel ashamed of myself for feeling that way. 1 2 3 4 5

12. When I am upset, I take time to figure out what I'm really feeling. 1 2 3 4 5

Highest Score = 12   Your Score _____

Step 3: Mental Stress

Directions: For each question choose from the following alternatives:

1) Never 2) Almost Never 3) Sometimes 4) Often 5) Very Often

1. In the last month, how often have you been upset because of something that happened unexpectedly? 1 2 3 4 5

2. In the last month, how often have you felt that you were unable to control the important things in your life? 1 2 3 4 5

3. In the last month, how often have you felt stressed? 1 2 3 4 5

4. In the last month, how often have you felt confident about your ability to handle your personal problems? 1 2 3 4 5

5. In the last month, how often have you found that you could not cope with all the things that you had to do? 1 2 3 4 5

6. In the last month, how often have you been able to control irritations in your life? 1 2 3 4 5

7. In the last month, how often have you felt that you were on top of things? 1 2 3 4 5

8. In the last month, how often have you felt difficulties were piling up so high that you could not overcome them? 1 2 3 4 5

Highest Score = 8   Your Score _____

Step 4: Other Discomforting Experiences

Instructions: Please read each statement and indicate on the scale below the degree to which you were BOTHERED by each symptom over the past month.

1) Never 2) Rarely 3) Sometimes 4) Often 5) Always

1. I felt depressed. 1 2 3 4 5

2. I felt sad. 1 2 3 4 5

3. I felt like a failure. 1 2 3 4 5

4. I felt that I had nothing to look forward to. 1 2 3 4 5

5. I felt anxious. 1 2 3 4 5

6. I found it hard to focus on anything other than my anxiety. 1 2 3 4 5

7. I felt nervous. 1 2 3 4 5

8. I felt like I needed help for my anxiety 1 2 3 4 5

9. I was irritated more than people knew. 1 2 3 4 5

10. I felt angry. 1 2 3 4 5

11. I felt like I was ready to explode. 1 2 3 4 5

12. I felt annoyed. 1 2 3 4 5

Highest Score = 12   Your score ____

Step 5: Mental Well-Being

Instructions: Below are some statements about feelings and thoughts. Using the scale below, please check the number that best describes your **typical experience** of each item:

1) None of the time 2) Rarely 3) Some of the time 4) Often 5) All of the time

1. I've been feeling optimistic about the future. 1 2 3 4 5

2. I've been feeling useful. 1 2 3 45

3. I've been feeling relaxed. 1 2 3 4 5

4. I've been feeling interested in other people. 1 2 3 4 5

5. I've had energy to spare. 1 2 3 4 5

6. I've been dealing with problems well. 1 2 3 4 5

7. I've been thinking clearly. 1 2 3 4 5

8. I've been feeling good about myself. 1 2 3 4 5

9. I've been feeling close to other people. 1 2 3 4 5

10. I've been feeling confident. 1 2 3 4 5

11. I've been able to make up my own mind about things. 1 2 3 4 5

12. I've been feeling loved. 1 2 3 45

13. I've been interested in new things. 1 2 3 4 5

14. I've been feeling cheerful. 1 2 3 45

Highest Score = 70 Your Score ____

Discussion

The purpose of these items is to help you gauge your present level of understanding of the Three Principles, the power of Thought, the power of innate mental health, and the extent to which you use the power of Thought in your best interest. Let's examine how you fared on these items. How often did you select the 6-point "Agree or Disagree Completely/No Exceptions" choice for the first survey? Remember, Principles, once discovered, explain everything—*no exceptions!* How did you score on the four short surveys measuring your typical use of the power of Thought? How did you do on the mental stress survey? Finally, how did you fare on the mental well-being items? Hopefully, your responses to these items will help you gauge your present level of understanding, *via insight,* of who you (and the rest of us) really are—*The Three Principles in action!*

It's important to recognize that mental health includes the ability to recognize symptoms of the "mental flu;" to understand their value, and how to relate to these symptoms in a way that diffuses their power—hastens their passing—prevents them from becoming "mental pneumonia." This is called *resilience—the ability to bounce back from painful feelings and discomforting states of mind.* In my view, resilience is where the "rubber meets the road" regarding flourishing mental health. Everyone functions quite well when they experience peace of mind, well-being, and common sense. However, absent the understandings that foster resilience—all it takes is one painful mood for people to seriously "muck up" their lives.

Unfortunately, most people have a slew of misguided beliefs about emotional pain. For example, many people believe that it's helpful, even essential, to experience painful feelings like stress, anger, anxiety, and depression. Many people believe that experiencing discomforting feelings helps build character and resilience. How often have you or someone you know said something like, "You can't appreciate the good feelings unless you experience the painful ones!"

Many people—including many mainstream psychologists—believe that painful feelings get stored up in people's minds where they silently fester and eventually erupt or explode. I used to think that people had to focus on their painful feelings—fully experience them—release them—get them out! I thought that people had to "get in touch with" their "inner pain" to be free of it. As a beginning therapist, I encouraged many clients to cry—let out their anger—resurrect painful memories. I thought that uncovering and purging painful emotions was essential for therapeutic success. Back then, when a client left my office in tears, I hoped one of my colleagues would notice and think, "What good work Dr. Kelley is doing!"

For years I was a prisoner of these misguided beliefs about painful feelings. Today, it's hard for me to believe that I used to glorify painful feelings—see them as a way to move people toward improved mental health. When my understanding of the Three Principles was insufficient, I couldn't see painful feelings for what they really are. Unless these discomforting feelings help us respond more effectively to a real and present danger—say a Greyhound bus about to flatten us—the purpose of painful feelings is to inform us that we are misusing the power of Thought and likely "accidents waiting to happen." *Stressful, painful, insecure, discomforting feelings are "wake-up calls" from Universal Mind trying to inform us that our thinking is skewed, or off-kilter and that we have drifted away from our innate health/common sense.*

Are you beginning to see the value of understanding the truth about feelings? Feelings are a built-in barometer of the quality of our thoughts, our state of mind, our mental health in the moment. Our feelings faithfully inform us whether we are using the power of Thought in our best interest or against ourselves! In the same way that physical discomfort alerts us that something is wrong with our body, painful feelings alert us that something is wrong with our thinking. Innate human feelings (e.g., well-being, exhilaration, gratitude, love) are a "green light" informing us that we are operating at or close to our best. Painful feelings like stress, anxiety, depression, envy, jealousy, and anger are "red lights" signaling us to slow down and allow our personal mind to relax.

When people have an insufficient understanding of painful feelings, they tend to be bothered by them—take them to heart—over-analyze them—get upset with themselves for experiencing them. Unfortunately, the more attention people pay to discomforting feelings, the more intense these feelings become and the longer they stick around. In the words of Roger Mills:

> "...as we begin to understand the real significance behind what we feel, we begin to realize that our feelings are an internal compass that can guide us past the pitfalls in life, regardless of the details or conditions that exist around us. Natural feelings let us know that our thinking is of higher quality and that we are moving in the right direction. If we feel negative, hostile, or depressed, it's time to step back and relax, to suspend struggle and judgments. If we wait patiently and allow our mind to clear, the common sense of wisdom will shine through the clouds and our thinking will be healthy once again."

A DEEPER DIVE

On YouTube watch or listen:

3PGC – How Getting Comfortable Being Uncomfortable Changed My Life: Rohini Ross

All Feelings Including the Good Ones Come from Thought: An Audio with Valda Monroe

CHAPTER 9

Some Advantages of Understanding the Three Principles

You have now been exposed (or exposed again) to the Three Principles that explain the way everyone's psychological life is created. Now you realize that everyone is experiencing a psychological life created "through them" from the "inside-out" via their use of the Principles of Thought + Consciousness—all powered up by Universal Mind. Now you "see" that thought is the only "reality" that people can ever know, and that people can recognize this fact and be conscious of it in the moment. Now you understand the way the power of Thought is meant to be used—innate health (i.e., Universal Mind) the master—personal/conceptual/analytical thought the faithful servant.

Now you realize that everyone has all the mental health they need already inside them—that the time people spend experiencing this health increases as the attention they pay to their personal thoughts—particularly their discomforting personal thoughts—decreases. You also realize that people's feelings serve as an internal barometer of the quality of their thoughts/state of mind/mental health in the moment. Now you understand that you, me, all of us are—*the Three Principles in action!* With these new insights, your hands are planted more firmly on the steering wheel of your psychological life. What follows are a few of the many advantages of grasping a sufficient insight-based understanding of the Three Principles.

The Quality of Our Present Moments

The present is all we ever have. What is it that determines the quality of our "successive moments of now?" That's right—it's our use of the Three Principles. What are our present moments like when we trust our innate health (i.e., Universal Mind) to guide us? As the master of our psychological lives, Universal Mind provides us with fresh, wise, insightful thoughts—rich, satisfying, natural feelings and unconditional self-esteem—and prompts regarding when to use personal thinking. When we trust our innate health to guide us, we experience richer, more satisfying present moments, and maintain well-being during discomforting "thought attacks" and challenging life experiences. Mental health/well-being/wisdom/resilience is built into everyone. This health can never be damaged and will never wear out. This health is buoyant—like a cork floating in water—constantly bobbing above the surface—unless we choose to weigh it down via misusing the power of Thought. George Pransky described the profound utility of this innate health:

> "To repeat and emphasize the central point: the Three Principles assert that [innate health] is available to all people, always, as a way of life. This health is a birthright. [It] provides the feelings people want for themselves. It provides a transcendent intelligence for problem-solving. It provides a clear [personal] mind so that people can have an uncontaminated view of life to enjoy the moment. It even provides us with prompts about when to use [personal] thinking. [It] is free from chronic stress and distress. It enables our humanity to come through in our personal relationships. [Innate mental health] is the most undiscovered and unappreciated resource in human existence."

Now you realize how to allow the power of Thought to operate in your best interest. When you trust Universal Mind to guide you in and out of personal thought, you are in store for a more flourishing life. On the other hand, if you think you can out smart Universal Mind—and allow personal thought to run your psychological life—you will innocently end up like I used to be—another person living with symptoms of the "mental flu"—searching and coping.

A DEEPER DIVE

On YouTube watch:

Living in the Now with Dr. Judy Sedgeman

The Missing Link Chapter 10 – Living in the Now: Bill Pettit & Judy Sedgeman

---

Free Will

We can't stop thoughts (painful, neutral, pleasant) from coming to mind. As long as we are alive, thoughts will keep on coming to mind. It's the only game in town. However, just because a thought enters your mind doesn't mean that it's your thought—doesn't mean it's true—doesn't mean you must honor it, entertain it, believe it. We all have *free will—the power to choose the thoughts we take seriously and entertain, and the thoughts we take with a grain of salt and allow to pass through.* In each moment, there are thousands of thoughts that can enter one's mind. This is where our *free will* comes in to play. In their Three Principles-based book, "Coming Home," Dicken Bettinger and Natasha Swerdloff describe free will this way:

> "Free will is like the steering wheel on a car. For example, if you are driving down the road and there is a big pothole in front of you, it makes sense to steer around it. You wouldn't think you need to go into it just to experience it. Using your free will allows your mind to open to new thinking. It doesn't mean you are denying what you were experiencing. When you take attention off what you are thinking, your mind opens up to new thinking."

A DEEPER DIVE

On YouTube watch:

The Concept of Free Will: Dicken Bettinger

The Illusion of Permanent Damage from Trauma

For over 30 years, I taught a graduate class at Wayne State University on child abuse and neglect. Every semester, I encountered "experts" who claimed that child victims of severe neglect or abuse are permanently "damaged." These so-called experts asserted that throughout life, these children must fight depression, anxiety, and rage—will rarely, if ever, experience warm, trusting, intimate relationships—and, as adults, will be prone to neglect or abuse their own children.

It's shameful that so many children experience horrid acts of abuse and neglect typically perpetrated by their trusted caregivers. However, it's helpful to realize that what many mainstream psychologists call "emotional scars" are merely painful memories etched into the minds of these children. However, these memories have no power to damage the mental health of these children unless they "think they do."

Feelings don't get stored in memory—only thoughts! We can't stop painful memories from coming to mind. I wish we could, but we can't—unless we go unconscious which has its drawbacks. However, once a painful memory surfaces—we have a choice. That's when our "free will" comes into play. We choose whether to entertain these memories or drop them.

The late psychologist, Wayne Dyer, told the following story about a young woman who was raped, beaten, and left to die in her disabled car on the edge of a desolate country road. Another car drove by and stopped. To her horror, this "hoped for" Good Samaritan raped her again and shot her in the head! Clinging to life by a thread, she was rescued and rushed to a hospital. Although she eventually recovered, she was blinded by the gunshot! Months later, while recuperating in her hospital room, a visitor was livid, seething with anger about what happened to his friend. The "victim," however, was at peace and hopeful about her future. Her positive demeanor upset her visitor even more and he finally exclaimed, "How can you be so calm. If I were you, I'd be bitter for the rest of my life!" The woman replied compassionately, "I know how much you care, but I see it this way. I gave those two men thirty minutes of my life. I'm not going to give them one second more!" Sydney Banks said, "… thoughts have no power of their own, only that which you give them."

A DEEPER DIVE

On YouTube watch:

PTSD and Trauma: Bill Pettit

PODCAST:

Psychology Has It Backwards, Episode #8: Can We Get Beyond Trauma

---

Personal Accountability and the End of Blame

Every experience we have is created by our use of the Three Principles—particularly our use of the power of Thought. It's always an "inside-out" job. Realizing this fact, allows people to be fully accountable for their psychological experiences and behaviors. Dicken Bettinger and Natasha Swerdloff described it this way:

> "Whatever you are feeling is always and only determined by how you use the Principles. You no longer feel like a victim of circumstance or people. You no longer feel insecure, vulnerable, and defensive. You feel secure because you no longer misunderstand where your feelings are coming from."

When people have a sufficient understanding of the Three Principles, they realize that blaming themselves and/or others for past actions is foolish. Why? Because they "see" that everyone is always doing the best they can, in the moment, based on how their thoughts make their lives appear to them. They realize that, in each moment, everyone is behaving in perfect harmony with the melody of their thoughts. This is a psychological fact! It's true for you, your parents, your ex-wife, your boss, your friends, your children, your siblings—everyone!

When people have a sufficient insight-based understanding of the Three Principles, they let themselves and others off the hook regarding the past. They stop blaming themselves and/or others for past actions—no matter how foolish. They "see" that blaming—dwelling on—reliving the past weighs down their mental health cork and contaminates their precious moments of now. When people trust their innate health to guide them—the past stays where it belongs—in the past.

A DEEPER DIVE

On YouTube watch:

Single Paradigm: Negative Self-Judgements and Self-Blame (from the Inside-Out)

The End of Coping

When people don't realize that the source of chronic emotional pain is their own innocent misuse of the power of Thought, they begin searching "out there" for ways to cope with their discomforting feelings and unsettling perceptions. Roger Mills put it this way:

"This manipulation could include hitting your spouse or children, picking a fight with someone, cheating, stealing, or otherwise trying to gain more control of your situation any way you can, or it could include drinking and using drugs. It could include self-pity as an attempt to feel better or obtain sympathy. It could include violence or lashing out verbally at others. It could include escaping into an inner world through delusional states or hallucinations...The common denominator across all these self-destructive habits is that each is what the person has learned to do, or feel is the best they can do, when they are caught in the grip of [stress and] insecurity."

These, and myriad other "coping strategies" are the best ways that people can see at the time to minimize their psychological pain when they don't realize its source and how to "nip it in the bud." However, when people grasp a sufficient understanding of the Three Principles, they realize that misusing the power of Thought is the only source of psychological pain, and they understand how to avoid it rather than searching "out there" for sources of temporary relief.

Problems, Needs, and Urges

Problems, needs, and urges are more apparitions that appear real to people who have an insufficient understanding of the Principles and the "inside-out" creation of psychological experiences. When people entertain stressful thoughts, life can seem problematic, unmanageable, even overwhelming. When people "squeeze" stressful thoughts, anything can appear to be a problem. When my thoughts are stressful, my condo looks like an old "money pit," my students seem dull and boring, and my writing becomes a struggle. However, when my personal mind quiets, my "problems" dissolve. Suddenly, I have a warm, comfortable condo—my students seem smarter and more interesting—my writing flows.

When people's personal minds clear, their problem mirages disappear! In the free-flowing stream of effortless intelligent thoughts, problems get transformed and become more manageable—even interesting challenges. When people stop taking their "problem thoughts" to heart, they are not in denial—they are simply recognizing and discounting the discomforting thoughts that create "problem mirages" in the first place.

Most needs, like problems, are also illusions. Unfortunately, most people tend to view life from an "outside-in" perspective and often innocently use the power of Thought against themselves. It isn't surprising, therefore, that most people think that in order to flourish, their needs must be met. They misguidedly think that flourishing is tied to "stuff out there"—their spouse making them feel loved and important—their employer satisfying their "financial needs"—the government supplying them with entitlements. Thus, they often feel needy and dependent and spend much of their lives struggling to get their needs met.

When people understand the Three Principles, however, the illusion of needs—except for some food, water, and shelter—evaporates. People realize that well-being doesn't depend on "stuff out there." Of course, people still see things "out there" they want, but they don't live in the illusion that they "need" these things to flourish. They recognize the discomforting feelings of neediness, insecurity, and dependency for what they really are—products of their own personal thinking. They are set free from the vicious cycle of believing and re-thinking discomforting personal thoughts—feeling needy and dependent—struggling to get their "needs" met—blaming themselves and/or others when they aren't.

You got it—it works the same way for urges. Urges are seductive, personal thoughts that come to mind for everyone—particularly during low moods—that tempt people to engage in various—often health-damaging—coping behaviors. Smoking, binge eating, gambling, drug abuse, and violence are behaviors that many people use to quiet their urge-thoughts. When people gain a sufficient understanding of the Three Principles, however, they realize they are not "damaged," "bad" or "sick" because they have been seduced in the past by urge-thoughts. Instead, they recognize that the methods they used in the past to cope, no matter how foolish, were the best ways they could see at the time to quiet their personal mind and mute their painful feelings.

A DEEPER DIVE

PODCASTS:

Sydney Banks - Solving Problems from the Inside-Out

Psychology Has It Backwards, Episode #23—Self, Ego, and Other Illusions

Psychology Has It Backwards, Episode #48—Dealing with Problems

Ask Amy: How Do I Dismiss Urges to Binge Eat and Cope with Everything Else in My Life

Understanding "Difficult" People

Why is it so difficult for most people to keep their bearings when they encounter a "difficult" person? When a "difficult" person treats them in a disrespectful way, why do so many people get so "bent out of shape?" For one thing, most people don't understand why certain people tend to be "difficult." Most people don't realize the source of "difficult" behavior in its myriad forms and flavors. This innocent misunderstanding has most people take others' "difficult" behavior personally. They innocently perceive the misguided behavior of "difficult" people as a slap at their self-worth. They think, "If I don't stand up to these people—I'll get "conned" or be seen as a "doormat" or a "wimp."

Scads of seminars, workshops, and books purport to teach people how to deal with "difficult" people. Some promote the idea that people have a right to feel hurt and angry when a "difficult" person treats them badly. Others posit that people should express their anger to these "bullies" in a civil, constructive way. Some posit that people should treat "difficult" people in the same obnoxious way they treat them. Millions have learned various methods to deal with "difficult" people. Yet, even armed with these tools and techniques, most people continue to get "stressed out" when a "difficult" person has them in their crosshairs.

When people understand the Three Principles, however, dealing with "difficult" people becomes easier. Why? Because when people get clear about the "inside-out" creation of everyone's psychological experiences, they realize the truth about "difficult" people. They "see" that these people are experts at misusing the power of Thought! Difficult people typically view life through biased, insecure thoughts and beliefs they think are "the truth." Then they misguidedly behave into the biased realities created by these thoughts and beliefs.

When people have a sufficient understanding of the Three Principles, however, they realize that the behavior of "difficult" people isn't personal. Thus, when they find themselves in the maladaptive-thinking spotlight of such people, they typically "see" that their actions have no power to hurt or damage them—unless they think they do.

How should you respond to a "difficult" person? What if one is your boss? What if you are married to one? What if one is your child, your parent, your sister, your in-law? Well, how about trusting your innate wisdom to show you a way that makes sense in the moment. Trust me—you will realize a wise response if your personal mind is quiet enough to hear it. When your ego quiets down, you can count on your inner wisdom—and your inner compassion—to guide you. If your ego-thoughts kick in and it starts to look personal, you can do your best to quiet down and give your innate wisdom some room to kick in before you act.

When people realize the truth about the way we all work psychologically, they stop worrying about how other people might treat them. Why? Because they recognize that it's never personal—that their well-being/self-esteem isn't in the hands of other people's opinions and actions. Also, they are more likely to experience compassion for people who are *innocently* living at the mercy of their misguided personal thoughts. Of course, they still take care of themselves and get out of the way of "difficult" people when it makes sense to do so.

A DEEPER DIVE

On YouTube watch:

A Whole New Way of Dealing with Difficult People: Michael Neil

Jack Pransky: The Best Kept Secret in Well-Being

Forgiveness

At age 10, Chris Carrier was abducted near his Florida home, taken into the swamps, stabbed repeatedly in the chest and abdomen with an ice pick, and then shot through the temple with a handgun. Remarkably, hours later, he awoke with a headache, unable to see out of one eye. He stumbled to the highway and stopped a car, which took him to the hospital. Years later, a police officer told Chris that the man suspected of his abduction lay close to death. "Confront him," suggested the officer. Chris did more than that. He comforted his attacker during the man's final weeks of life and ultimately forgave him, bringing peace to them both. Consider these sentiments from Adam Cohen:

> "Imagine all the ways that people appear to hurt or annoy each other in a day. The barista at the coffee house took too long to make your latte and then used low-fat milk, instead of regular, as you ordered. When you finally got the right coffee and drove off in your car, someone cut you off in traffic, making you spill your latte on yourself. All of this happened on your birthday, which your best friend forgot. As a matter of fact, the coffee-stained shirt was a birthday present from this same friend two years ago. You can imagine that such a day might test whether you are prone to ruminate and be angry, or whether you tend to forgive. If we didn't forgive people for any of these hurts, real or imagined, our lives would be filled with anger and spite. We might spend our time plotting and carrying out revenge and avoiding people that we really ought to be close to.

Forgiveness can free us from this kind of life. It allows people to live together and get on with their lives. It is one of the most important factors in promoting peace between people, and well-being."

Numerous studies show that forgiveness can reap huge rewards for one's physical health as well—lowering the risk of heart attack, improving cholesterol levels and sleep; reducing pain and blood pressure as well as levels of anxiety, depression, and stress. The longer people hold onto grudge-thoughts, the more chance they have of developing a heart-related disorder. Research also points to an increase in the forgiveness-health connection as people age. Dicken Bettenger and Natasha Swerdloff put it this way:

"Realizing [the power of] Thought keeps you from believing that anything other than thought is creating your stress. You stop blaming other people for your discomfort or upset. You stop believing that the weather can determine the way you feel, or that someone can make you feel good or bad. You stop blaming the world for your experience… You also learn to forgive yourself by seeing your own innocence… Whatever you are feeling is always and only determined by how you use the Principles."

A DEEPER DIVE

On YouTube watch:

Sydney Banks: Forgive Yourself

Forgiveness and the Three Principles with Tyler Thurman

Dicken Bettinger on Forgiveness

PODCASTS:

Psychology Has It Backwards, Episode #15—Psychological Innocence: The Foundation of Forgiveness

Psychology Has It Backwards, Episode #16—Forgive Yourself; Forgive Others

A Low-Stress Life

People have loads of misguided ideas about stress. Most people believe that if you actively participate in life—stress is inevitable. Most people think, "Life is tough, and along with the good stuff comes the stress." The common belief that people must cope with life assumes that life is inherently stressful. Retirement is supposed to be that glorious time when people finally get rid of their stress and start "really living." Yet, many companies offer their prospective retirees seminars on coping with retirement stress!

Most people believe that the source of stress is "out there" in the circumstances, events, and actions of other people. There is work stress caused by job duties and supervisors—relationship stress caused by partners and children—holiday stress caused by shopping and partying—post-traumatic stress caused by adverse life events. The list of stressors gets longer every year. How about seasonal affective disorder or SAD—stress caused by gloomy weather!

It's as if "little stress particles" are attached to stuff out there. If you get too close—they stick to you and "zap"—you're stressed! Psychologists have developed scales on which you get "stress points" for enduring certain life challenges like a job change, a new mortgage, or a divorce. The more stress points you accumulate, the more likely you are to get sick or have an accident in the near future. Most people believe these misguided ideas about stress and most mornings they wake up to a "stressful" world.

When people understand the Three Principles, however, they "see" that the one and only source of stress is stressful thoughts. More importantly, they realize that stress is their friend—an internal alarm alerting them that they are using the power of Thought against themselves. Stress doesn't come from "stuff out there." There are only stressful thoughts, and they are not happening out there. Life isn't stressful. Your mother-in-law isn't stressful. Your clients aren't stressful. Your boss isn't stressful. Winter isn't stressful. Even a bad hair day isn't stressful! There are no "stressors" out there. Yes, bad things happen to good people. However, our experience of the events, circumstances, and the people we encounter is created solely via our understanding and use of the power of Thought.

A DEEPER DIVE

On YouTube watch:

The Real Source of Stress with George Pransky

Michael Neil—An End to Stress (3 Parts)

PODCASTS:

Psychology Has It Backwards, Episode #21—Burn-Out

Psychology Has It Backwards, Episode #56—Stress is Not a Thing

---

Effortless Change

I'm writing this in late December. Every year around this time, millions of people make New Year's resolutions—promises to change their lives in myriad ways—lose weight, quit smoking, eat healthier, exercise more, change jobs, get more education, improve relationships, build self-esteem, reduce stress, and on and on. By March, however, most will give up—many with broken promises and feelings of guilt and failure. Others will "work their fannies off" and—at least for a while—fulfill their resolutions. Yet, for most of these "successful people" making these changes will be a struggle—even drudgery!

Why does this "resolution/failure ritual" continue year after year? Well, for most people, the motivation for change comes from the misguided belief that altering "stuff out there" will lead to more happiness. Sounds a lot like that "more, better, different" game we visited earlier, doesn't it? When people don't realize that they already have all the mental health they need inside them, they try to find it by doing "more/better/different" stuff out there. And guess what—in the long run, it never works!

Change motivated by this "outside-in" belief system is never deeply satisfying and typically requires constant effort and maintenance. Even if people keep their resolutions, change motivated by ego—rather than well-being and wisdom—tends to be harsh, hollow, and burdensome. That's why so many well-intentioned people give up—why so many people make the same resolutions—New Year after New Year.

When people understand the Three Principles, however, they realize that change spawned via wisdom is more natural and easier. When people trust their innate health to guide them, their motivators du jour include curiosity, inspiration, and common sense. Via trusting their innate health to direct them, people realize what makes sense to change and do what's called for in a more natural, free-flowing way. Don't get me wrong—change spawned by wisdom often takes considerable effort. However, "effort" is experienced in a more "effortless way" by people who are already flourishing.

A DEEPER DIVE

PODCASTS:

Psychology Has It Backwards, Episode 62: New Year's Inspirations vs. Resolutions

Psychology Has It Backwards Episode #32: Changing Gracefully

The Secret of Effortless Change with Michael Neill

Freedom that Lasts: The No-Willpower Approach to Breaking Any Habit

Leaving the Past Where It Belongs

When people understand the Three Principles, they realize that the "past" and the "future" are more thought-created illusions. All we ever have is the present—successive moments of now. We all live in the present; we have no other choice. We do have a choice, however, about how we experience our precious present moments. Painful memories can get transported into the present and there's nothing we can do about it. However, once these memories take form—we choose how we relate to them. If we relate to painful memories in the same way we relate to a "nightmare," these memories have no power. Think about it—when you awaken from a nightmare and realize it was "just a nightmare," you are fine. You don't waste your day ruminating about the nightmare and searching for places to hide from the zombies. You simply disregard it and get on with your life.

When people live in, dwell on, and won't "let go" of the past, they misguidedly contaminate their present moments. They spend scads of their present moments entertaining thoughts like, "It was so much better back then," "I'll never be as happy as I was in the good old days," "My mother loved my brother more than me," and "I'll never forgive my father for abandoning me." When people understand the Three Principles, however, they see that chronically re-thinking discomforting thoughts weighs down their mental health cork and contaminates their precious moments of now. When people trust the present moment (Universal Mind) to guide them, the past stays where it belongs—in the past.

A DEEPER DIVE

On YouTube watch:
  Bill Pettit - Built to Fly

Effortless Relationships

How would relationships evolve if everyone had a sufficient understanding of the way the Three Principles create our psychological lives—that thought is the only experience that people can ever know—that everyone has all the mental health they need already inside them. What if everyone understood these facts and were as clear about them as they are that the

Earth is round? What would relationships be like if people were 100% accountable for their psychological experiences and behaviors—stopped blaming circumstances and other people for their upsets—stopped depending on others to get their needs met—saw the innocence in the "difficult" behavior of other people—realized the value of forgiveness—and trusted their innate health (i.e., Universal Mind) to direct their lives?

Question: How would relationships change if everyone understood the "inside-out" creation of everyone's psychological experiences and the fact of separate realities?

Possibility: The fact that everyone lives in a separate reality and sees life differently would be accepted as a simple truth.

Question: What difference would that make for relationships?

Possibility: The fact that everyone sees life differently would no longer be confusing or threatening to people. It would be seen as normal, interesting—even fascinating.

Question: What difference would that make for relationships?

Possibility: People would stop fighting with each other to prove that their personal reality was right or "the truth."

Question: What difference would that make for relationships?

Possibility: People would typically relate with others from natural human feelings like well-being, exhilaration, curiosity, compassion, and love.

Question: What difference would that make for relationships?

Possibility: Relationships would be more intimate, creative, productive, wise, cooperative, flexible, trustworthy, and compassionate.

Question: What difference would that make for relationships?

Possibility: People would work together in more cooperative, common-sense ways and uncover wise solutions for vexing problems like poverty, crime, hunger, and climate change.

Question: What difference would that make for relationships?

Possibility: _____

_____

_____

Please add your vision here!

A DEEPER DIVE

On YouTube watch:

Tom Kelley Interview with Lori Carpenos

The Most Important Things about Relationships with George & Linda Pransky

Relationships and the Three Principles: with Michael Neill

PODCASTS:

The Secret to Feeling More in Love with Your Spouse: with Michael Neil

Psychology Has It Backwards, Episode #25—Moods and Relationships

BOOK:

The Relationship Handbook by George & Linda Pransky

PART V

Teaching the Three Principles

CHAPTER 10

Three Principles Mental Health Education

Three Principles psychologist, Roger Mills, summarized the events following Sydney Banks's uncovering of the Three Principles:

"The first several years following [Sydney Banks's] discovery were spent on deepening our appreciation for the implications of this understanding. The operational Principles and the underlying logic revealed by them were so unique, they stood out as distinctly different from previous assumptions and theories underlying most treatment programs, of mental health interventions, and of educational, leadership, motivational, and social change programs. These Principles shifted our view of human nature and our most basic psychic functioning to an extent that a new framework for understanding the source of mental health and a new intervention methodology had to be developed from scratch. The basic premises, ideas, and active ingredients introduced by these Principles simply did not exist in the previous literature. Thus, the practice of both therapy and prevention based on these Principles required completely new ways of listening, conducting assessment, and teaching or interviewing."

Sydney Banks described the power of Thought as "the missing link between mental sickness and mental health." Unfortunately, most people have insufficient insight regarding the way the Principles of Universal Mind, Consciousness, and Thought create everyone's psychological experiences. Absent a sufficient insight-based understanding of these Principles, people are prone to innocently misuse the power of Thought and thereby to create chronic mental stress and obscure or cover over their natural state of mental well-being.

However, people can be assisted to recognize, in the moment, that what they are experiencing is a temporary manifestation created by their use of the Three Principles. If people do not realize this fact, they will tend to take their personal thoughts to heart and act on whatever "reality" these thoughts create. However, when people recognize this fact, they will be less likely to view their personal thoughts—particularly their discomforting personal thoughts—as "the truth" or the way things really are—and less likely to act on them.

People can also be assisted to see what they experience when they fall into the present moment and what they feel like at those times. They can be assisted to see that only their misuse of the power of Thought can get in the way of this natural, healthy state. When people gain a sufficient, insight-based understanding of the Three Principles, recognize the inextricable connection between their thoughts and their psychological experiences, realize the power and ready availability of innate mental health—and can access this understanding in the moment—the common precursor to psychopathology will plummet.

In sum, the common liability in all forms of psychopathology is an insufficient, insight-based understanding of the Principles of Universal Mind, Consciousness, and Thought. Another way of seeing this is that people come into the world in a state of pure consciousness (i.e., fully immersed in the moment) and experiencing innate mental health. However, absent a sufficient understanding of the Three Principles, people innocently learn to overuse and misuse the power of Thought and chronically cover over or obscure this innate health. Sydney Banks stated:

"[Everyone] is subject to what I would call psychological viruses... such as greed, hate, jealousy, desire, and envy just to name a few... such viruses are as natural as breathing and nobody journeys through this life completely immune from them. When you are suffering from such a virus, you are not sick per se... you are temporarily and innocently not thinking straight."

Mental Health Education

Practitioners of the Three Principles understanding (or 3P practitioners) typically view themselves as teachers or *mental health educators*. This education has as its goal awakening people's understanding of the "inside-out" creation of people's psychological experiences via their use of the Three Principles. This education assumes that people have an intuitive understanding of the Universal Truths to which the Three Principles point and that this awareness can be awakened. Thus, this is a process of recognition and realization; in contrast to feeding information to the personal intellect. Sydney Banks stated:

"[The Three Principles describe] ... the missing link between our psychological nature and our spiritual nature... As we start to regain the true relationship between our personal intelligence and the spiritual wisdom that lies within, we develop a higher degree of intelligence and common sense. This, in turn, clears up our misguided lives."

Effective 3P Practitioners

Effective 3P practitioners have a sufficient understanding, via insight, of the way the Three Principles manifest within everyone—have applied this insight to their own lives with improved results—and generally live in a state of well-being themselves. 3P practitioners focus on the innate health in their clients, as opposed to focusing on the external, illness, diagnosis, or problematic behaviors. They do not view even the most troubled people as damaged or in need of fixing. Instead, they see them as whole and complete. While this practice is free form, in that there are no specific techniques, it is founded on the "health of the helper," the unconditional faith of 3P practitioners in the health of their clients, and practitioners' ability to listen deeply and trust their own wisdom to guide them.

3P practitioners attempt to draw out their clients' innate health from their own wisdom as they work with them. As they listen and respond, clients have their own insights and their innate health surfaces as they see for themselves that they are not damaged, can access natural well-being and wisdom, and are not prisoners of their own worse thoughts. Jack Pransky put it this way:

> "The primary difference between traditional forms of psychotherapy and Three Principles psychotherapy is that with traditional therapies, the feelings and problems people experience are considered real things that one can be helped to deal with constructively in many varying ways, depending on the therapy. In Three Principles therapy, the feelings and problems are considered to be essentially illusions or mirages created by one's power of Thought. The solution is to see these feelings and problems for the self-creations they truly are via new insight arising from wisdom... These new ways of thinking can only be realized through new insight (as opposed to cognitive restructuring)."

As people's insight-based understanding of the Three Principles deepens, they realize that their psychological experiences are created via the powers of Thought and Consciousness and are transient as their thoughts change. They recognize that every so-called reality is a fleeting, ephemeral product of their own minds at work. When people grasp the inextricable connection between their thoughts and their feelings, perceptions, states of mind, and behaviors, they gain perspective on life. Shifts in their experience show up as "thought events" rather than effects of past or present circumstances or how other people treat them. In turn, they are less likely to view their momentary thoughts and their manifestations as "the truth" or the way things really are, and to act indiscriminately on the "realities" this thinking creates. More importantly, they realize that beneath their discomforting thoughts, they are perfectly healthy, whole, and complete.

Everyone experiences negative thoughts and the discomforting experiences they create (e.g., lowered mood, increased anxiety, mental confusion). However, when people relate to these experiences as help-ful information about the quality of their thoughts, they are less likely to believe in the "reality" of those thoughts and to regain well-being and a fresh perspective. Through mental health education grounded in the Three Principles, people are assisted to realize that as they pay less attention to their discomforting personal thoughts—they become more present—and their "psychological viruses" evaporate. Put another way, people live more often "in the now." Sydney Banks stated:

> "When… people refer to the now, they mean the personal mind
> is free from the contaminants of yesterday's memories and fears.
> This in turn frees the mind to see with clarity things as they are,
> not through distorted memories and apprehensions…"

Preconditions for Change

Three Principles practitioners first attempt to establish and nurture the necessary preconditions for the change process to unfold. In Three Prin-ciples interventions, qualities of interaction are characterized by respect, seeing clients as equals, humor, empathy, compassion, engaging interac-tions, and by assuming their clients have inadvertently become caught up in certain habits of thinking, innocently forgetting that their habitual thoughts are not telling them the truth. 3P practitioners see their client's behavior, no matter how misguided, as the best they can do given how they have learned to think about life. As learners gain the experience of being at ease, relaxed, and playful, the pressure of their conditioned personal thoughts wears off. Their personal minds relax, and they become less self-conscious. These qualities of interaction allow learners to recognize their inherent integrity and reengage their innate health.

When this relaxed state is achieved, practitioners begin teaching about the Three Principles. They help learners recognize how the outcomes in every area of their lives are determined by the thoughts they bring to those situations. They show learners the link between the quality of their thoughts and their resulting perceptions and feelings. They assist learners to see the logical connection of their shifting states of mind with their mental well-being. They point out, in a way that learners can connect to their everyday experiences, the tendency of innate health to bubble up spontaneously when the debris of their discomforting thoughts clears.

3P learner's pasts, culture, education, job status, relationships, adverse experiences, and so forth are not the direct focus of the 3P intervention. As 3P practitioners assist their clients to realize and remove the smokescreen of their biased thoughts around these external factors, their capacity for wisdom and resilient functioning moves into the foreground. Three Principles practitioners realize that the more deeply clients tap into their own innate wisdom, they begin to "see" their own solutions for their "problems" and improve their functioning in these areas themselves.

Another aspect of this is seeing the innocence in their clients—that they are always doing their best, given their current thinking. When people break the law, are violent, abuse their partners or children, abuse drugs, and resist treatment, it is only because their thinking is "off" and they are not aware of it. They have no choice other than to act on what their thinking tells them because it looks so real to them—courtesy of consciousness. They don't "see" that their thinking is off-kilter, skewed. They are only following what they see. In this sense, they are innocent—they can't see anything else.

Seeing the innocence, however, does not mean denying that someone is causing harm to another or displaying a lack of conscience by their actions. If they did harm, if they broke the law, they may have to pay the consequences, but this has nothing to do with how they are seen by practitioners of this understanding. Within their world views, people can justify anything they think and do. When people act destructively, they are simply unable to see beyond their own creations that, to them, appear "real." Sydney Banks stated:

". . . a lost thinker experiences isolation, fear, and confusion… The misled thoughts of humanity, alienated from their innate wisdom, cause all violence, cruelty, and savagery in the world."

A DEEPER DIVE

Jack Pransky and I co-authored a paper that describes several guideposts typically followed by effective 3P practitioners. Our paper was published in the *Journal of Creativity in Mental Health* (Pransky & Kelley, 2014). A summary of these guideposts follows from Jack Pransky's book *Prevention from the Inside-Out*.

I. Modeling Mental Health

Effective Three Principles practitioners have gained sufficient insight-based understanding of the Principles themselves, have applied this understanding to their own lives with improved results, live their own lives from this "inside-out" perspective, and emanate mental well-being.

II. Creating a Climate for Insight-Based Learning

Essentially, effective 3P teachers help their clients' personal minds relax. From a relaxed mind, people are more likely to have new insights. This begins with how they see their clients—*which their clients can feel in return*. These practitioners realize that even their most disturbed clients have innate mental health. They see this health within every potential learner as opposed to seeing or focusing on the external, problematic behavior. They do not view even the most troubled client as damaged and in need of fixing with the right beliefs, skills, or techniques. Instead, they relate to them as their spiritual essence, *whole and complete*. They also see *the innocence in the learner's behavior,* no matter how disturbed, because they realize this misguided behavior is perfectly aligned with how the learner's personal thoughts make their life appear to them.

III. Deep Listening

Effective Three Principles practitioners listen via something akin to intuition, which allows them to pick up and realize how their clients create their realities, how their worlds look to them, how their current views may be obscuring their innate health, and what they may need to realize about the inside-out creation of people's psychological lives. It is listening more to what the client is not saying than to the words they are using. As such, it is the opposite of "active listening" where an effort is made to pay close attention to what the client is saying. By listening in a seemingly effortless way, 3P teachers see more clearly the way their learner's innate health is being obscured by their personal thoughts and what they need to realize to stop believing these thoughts and create space for this health to surface.

IV. Drawing-Out Three Principles Understanding

Once learners' personal minds relax and 3P teachers are listening deeply, the conditions are in place to help learners realize the innate health that lies within them and how they have obscured this health by innocently misusing the power of Thought. Basically, this involves conveying or "unveiling" what people already know. When 3P learners grasp these understandings, they see the truth about their circumstances—something of which their own minds create meaning and carry through time. When learners realize that emotional discomfort is a state of mind, the grip of their health-obscuring personal thoughts loosens, and they rebound to healthier states of mind more readily.

A DEEPER DIVE

On YouTube watch:

Living the Principles, Not Doing the Principles: Christine Heath and Judy Sedgeman

Teach What You Know of the Principles: Mark Howard

Coaching and the Three Principles: Michael Neill

How to REALLY Impact Your Coaching Clients: Dicken Bettinger

CHAPTER 11

How Three Principles Mental Health Education Differs From Mainstream Psychotherapies

It is essential to distinguish Three Principles mental health education from prominent mainstream psychotherapies, particularly cognitive behavioral therapy (CBT), with which it is often confused. Other than the use of the word "thought," Three Principles mental health education bears little resemblance to CBT. First, a man from outside the field of psychology had a spontaneous enlightenment experience where he realized the way the Three Principles work together to create people's psychological lives and then taught what he realized to mental health professionals. Thus, its development happened completely independent of CBT. Next, the Three Principles intervention focuses on *the power to think,* or "that people think" rather than thought content, or "what people think." If people only see "thoughts" rather than the "power of Thought" to bring them whatever thoughts/experiences they have, they will continually have to fight their maladaptive thoughts and schemas.

The intention of CBT may be summed up as helping people see that they can think differently about their discomforting thoughts, moods, and "real" life challenges. Unlike CBT, Three Principles education does not teach people to struggle with the content of their thinking. Instead, its dual goals may be summed up as: a) helping people see that their "problems" are illusions of their own creation; and b) that at their core, they already are perfectly mentally healthy and only their personal thoughts—believed and taken to heart—can make it appear that they are not. In summary, Three Principles mental health education is unique because of its neutral view of Thought as a creative power. CBT focuses on the content of the client's thinking as though there is an absolute reality about which the client can think differently. Three Principles education teaches that the "reality" people see and experience is itself their own thoughts.

Furthermore, unlike mindfulness-based interventions (e.g., mindfulness-based stress reduction; acceptance and commitment therapy), Three Principles education does not assist people in finding techniques to quiet the mind. Rather, it is about helping people realize that when they are not gripped by their personal thoughts, a more mindful state naturally appears. Put another way, when people's typical, day-to-day, or habitual personal thinking subsides, what is left is the quiet, and out of the quiet, people feel a sense of peace, or love, or feel one with the moment, or have new, wise insights from out of the blue. This state is the essence of who people truly are, and they can only stop experiencing this health via obscuring it with their own personal thoughts.

Several researchers including Jon Kabot-Zinn, Herbert Benson, Martin Seligman, and Mihalyi Csikszentmihalyi have generated and stimulated an enormous amount of research into the effects of practicing techniques to quiet the mind. However, people can realize less stress and improved mindfulness/flow/mental health as a lifestyle—without practicing techniques or coping strategies—via sufficient understanding of the "inside-out" creation of everyone's psychological experiences. Mindfulness/flow/well-being is people's most natural state, a buoyant state that surfaces spontaneously whenever people cease the only thing keeping this health covered over in the first place—their own innocent misuse of the power of Thought.

Awareness Versus Understanding

Many mainstream psychotherapies attempt to increase people's awareness of the content of their thinking (e.g., their beliefs, schemas). For these methods, *awareness* refers to a client's recognition of discomforting memories and biased beliefs, perhaps how they developed historically, and various techniques and tools to challenge and recondition these memories and beliefs. Three Principles practitioners, on the contrary, help people understand that everyone is continually using the powers of Thought and Consciousness to create their psychological experiences from the "inside-out." They strive to deepen their clients' understanding of Thought as a creative power used by everyone to experience thoughts that consciousness enlivens and gives the appearance of "reality." Thus, *understanding* in Three Principles mental health education is not about thought content or "what people think." Rather, understanding refers to the way Thought and Consciousness work from within to create people's psychological lives and how what people call "reality" is their own self-generated creation.

In this regard, renowned CBT practitioner and researcher John Teasdale, reported that assisting people to change how they relate to their negative thoughts and discomforting feelings—which Teasdale refers to as "de-centering"—may be more useful than teaching people techniques to modify or recondition their thoughts and beliefs. In other words, rather than viewing their thoughts as "the truth" or "reality," clients are helped to relate to them as merely "events in the mind." Teasdale concluded:

> "This perspective... represented a shift in our fundamental understanding. Previously, we, and others, had seen de-centering as one of a number of things going on in cognitive therapy. Our analysis suggested that it was central... If such de-centering did not take place, patients would be left arguing with themselves about whether their thoughts were true or not, marshalling evidence for or against a negative."

Three Principles education does not teach that practicing techniques (e.g., meditation) is a bad idea or should not be practiced. It simply offers an alternative view of what is behind what makes these techniques, interventions, and activities work for some, which might lead to a deeper understanding. Regarding meditation, for example, Dicken Bettinger and Natasha Swerdloff stated:

> "Realizing the Principles leads you to a natural meditative state. When you wake up to the fact of Thought, you stop being influenced by your personal thinking and you rest in the now… the meditative state is your natural state. It is always there but is covered over by your involvement in personal thinking. Meditation is not something you arrive at as a result of doing something. It is the essence of who you are."

Memory Work Versus Memory Recognition

Consider a client diagnosed with posttraumatic stress disorder or PTSD. A CBT counselor would attempt to help this person address the perceived traumatic event. This counselor would view the 'traumatic' event as a major focus of treatment, the client's fearful reaction to the event as a signal of proper therapeutic direction, and the client's PTSD symptoms as facts about which the client must learn to think more rationally or keep at bey with other techniques. The CBT counselor would then focus on the client's memories and beliefs regarding the traumatic event, as if these thoughts had power independent of the client thinking they do. Then the counselor would attempt to recondition the client's thinking as though it were a fixed experience, with little or no acknowledgment of the subtle variations in the client's thinking that coincide with an ever-changing state of mind.

A 3P practitioner, on the contrary, would view the client's "traumatic" memories as merely stored thoughts regarding the past enlivened by their consciousness and made to look real in the present. This practitioner would view the traumatic event in and of itself as having no special importance to the therapy process. Rather than focusing on the client's painful memories and teaching the client techniques to recondition these memories, the 3P counselor would teach that memories are simply thoughts brought forward from the past with present thinking and that the client can recognize these unproductive memories as thoughts, allow them to pass through and, by so doing, these thoughts and the painful feelings they spawn will be healed naturally via the intelligence of Universal Mind.

Coping with Feelings
Versus Understanding Feelings

Most mainstream psychotherapies focus directly on the client's discomforting feelings as if they had a life and influence of their own. These methods attempt to teach people ways to cope with these feelings, such as cognitive restructuring, conflict resolution, problem-solving, meditation, and anger management. In contrast, 3P practitioners recognize that if clients engage in techniques to manage negative feelings, these feelings are still acting on them because rather than being merely dismissible thoughts, they still appear real and to demand attention. 3P practitioners help clients understand that painful feelings are products of their own thinking—merely painful thoughts that have no power over them unless they think they do—and that they can relate to these discomforting thoughts/feelings as they would an unwanted memory, nightmare, or daydream.

Change via Techniques
Versus Transformation via Insight

Most mainstream counseling methods attempt to teach clients various techniques to help them recondition their negative thoughts and better cope with the discomforting feelings they spawn. In contrast, 3P teachers strive for more natural and sustained change, which will emerge from a sufficient, insight-based understanding of the Three Principles. For example, a client who tends to react violently and learns techniques to better manage anger would be seen by a 3P practitioner as preferable to a similar client with no positive improvement. However, the 3P practitioner would view this improvement as temporary and treatment as incomplete until the client realizes how anger is created by their own thoughts, minimizes the significance of the angry thoughts that make violence appear desirable, is living typically in a healthier state of mind, and is able to distinguish and correct for discomforting states of mind. In sum, a 3P practitioner would consider a violence-prone client able to function in society in a healthy way only when this client has grasped sufficient insight that minimizes the significance of the angry thoughts-feelings that previously preceded their violent behavior.

Teaching Health Versus Treating Illness

Most mainstream psychotherapies strive to treat diagnosed illnesses categorized in the *Diagnostic and Statistical Manual of Mental Disorders or DSM-V*. These methods assume that clients are restored to their "normal" level of health or highest previous "global level of functioning" when their presenting symptoms and problems appear to be relieved or resolved. In contrast, the primary goal of 3P mental health education is to facilitate a permanent, positive change in a client's overall mental health. 3P practitioners view a client's presenting symptoms as evidence of insufficient insight-based understanding of the Three Principles, the power of Thought, and the power of innate mental health.

A client's presenting symptoms are viewed compassionately and non-judgmentally by 3P practitioners. However, these symptoms are seen as irrelevant to effective intervention because 3P practitioners trust that as their clients gain sufficient understanding of the Three Principles, their symptoms will naturally resolve across the board. Thus, the Three Principles intervention differs markedly from CBT, mindfulness-based, and other prominent mainstream psychotherapies that attempt to put more well-being into people by reconditioning their beliefs, teaching them mind-quieting and other techniques, improving their communication, problem-solving, and coping skills, and inculcating positive virtues and character strengths. Rather, 3P practitioners assist their clients to realize, rekindle, and sustain the innate mental health that exists undamaged inside them.

In sum, Three Principles mental health education differs from CBT, mindfulness-based therapies, eye-movement desensitization reprocessing (EMDR), and other prominent mainstream psychotherapies that focus primarily on the content of people's thinking or "what people think." Rather, Three Principles mental health education focuses on the "fact of thought" or "that people think" and people's use of the power of Thought to create their psychological lives. Nor, like cognitive and emotionally oriented interventions, does 3P education attempt to supply people with tools, techniques, and strategies to help them recondition their dysfunctional beliefs, reframe a traumatic event, or better cope with painful feelings. Nor, like spiritually integrated interventions, does it incorporate spiritual or religious beliefs or concerns. Finally, the 3P intervention does not suggest that people create their life circumstances, nor that there is a fixed reality externally about which people should attempt to think differently. Rather, it suggests that in the same way that people continually use the Principle of gravity to stay planted on the ground, people continually use the Three Principles to create their experienced realities.

A DEEPER DIVE

Ken Manning and I co-authored a paper titled "Realizing the Power of Thought and Innate Mental Health: The Invisible Ingredients for Resolving Traumatic Memories." Our paper was published in the *Journal of Spirituality in Mental Health* (*Kelley & Manning, 2022*). The material that follows is based on our paper.

Trauma Resolution:
Why CBT Works When It Does

Cognitive-behavioral approaches to trauma resolution have three basic components: a) exposure to painful memories of the adverse event; b) cognitive restructuring of the assumptions and beliefs associated with the troubling memories and replacing them with more positive or rational thoughts; and c) skills training to improve the behavior of clients to be more adaptive and responsive to their current lives. Viewed through the lens of the Three Principles understanding, if these components succeed in reducing a client's distress, the reasons for this improvement are: a) the well-being experienced by the client during the counseling sessions (e.g., client-therapist relational trust) allows the client's personal mind to relax and create room for their innate health/wisdom to surface; and b) the focus on environmental cues during the sessions (e.g., positive thoughts, life skills development) distracts the client from their discomforting thoughts enough for them to realize that their relived sensory experiences are connected to thoughts coming to mind and that these discomforting thoughts are no longer relevant to the present moment. In other words, this realization enables the client to see their discomforting memories as thoughts. Sydney Banks put it this way:

> "I do not ask anyone to ignore their past experiences. This would be denial and denial is not a healthy state. Instead, seek a clearer understanding of the past; realize that negative feelings and emotions from past traumatic experiences are no longer true. They are merely memories, a collection of old, stale thoughts."

While CBT methods may help reduce the distress created via a client's painful memories, they typically do not result in sufficient insight-based understanding of the Three Principles, the power of Thought, and the power of innate mental health. Also, by encouraging clients to re-think painful memories, CBT therapists may be inadvertently reinforcing the idea that the past is living inside the person and that their discomforting experiences are not merely thoughts brought to life via consciousness. Thus, these components risk re-traumatizing the client in the service of healing and may compound the client's personal thinking regarding these troubling memories. Another potential problem is that CBT therapists do not typically assist their clients to see the importance of innate mental health (i.e., Universal Mind) as a part of natural trauma resolution and healthy living. Also, rather than focusing on the client's power to form thoughts, CBT focuses primarily on the client's thoughts after they are created.

Trauma Resolution: Why EMDR Works When It Does

Eye-movement desensitization reprocessing (EMDR) is purported to be quite successful and useful in a wide range of applications and has been hailed by many mainstream psychologists as a breakthrough in the field of trauma resolution. Its main procedures are as follows: a) the client engages in repetitive thought regarding the trauma and their negative beliefs associated with the adverse event; b) the therapist then moves some object (e.g., pencil, light) back and forth in front of the client and the client tracks the back and forth movements; c) the client is encouraged to re-think the discomforting thoughts and beliefs associated with the traumatic event, and then do further visual tracking; d) following reduction of the associated distress, the client rehearses positive beliefs designed to counteract the negative beliefs associated with the traumatic experience; and e) if other painful memories are revealed during the process, the same procedures are repeated.

Viewed through the Three Principles paradigm, when EMDR works, the main reason for its effectiveness is distraction. By asking the client to attend, in the moment, to sensory experiences other than the ones associated with the traumatic memories, the person is likely to realize, eventually, that these memories are not responsive in the moment but rather are products of their own mind. Rehearsing compensating positive beliefs along with further distraction (visual eye movement focusing) helps the client to see their painful memories as thoughts—not as living experiences with a force of their own. In other words, distraction facilitates the client seeing these memories as mental phenomena, rather than experiences to be re-lived in the moment, which allows the client's personal mind to quiet down and the natural trauma resolution process to engage.

There are aspects of EMDR, however, that may complicate the trauma resolution process for some clients. First, most EMDR therapists encourage their clients to focus on the traumatic event and its results rather than directly assisting them to recognize they are chronically re-thinking painful thoughts. Second, the client is encouraged to rehearse negative beliefs about the traumatic event without being encouraged to see these beliefs as thoughts. Third, the positive beliefs encouraged by the therapist may unwittingly anchor the client's negative beliefs for which they are intended to compensate. On the other hand, if a client's negative beliefs are treated as thoughts, it is easier for the client to dismiss them than if they are treated as realities from which a client is trying to flee. Fourth, the client is left with techniques for distracting themselves in the future without sufficient understanding of the powers of Thought and innate health that would allow them to dismiss these thoughts and allow the natural trauma resolution process to engage. Finally, if EMDR techniques should, at some point, fail to work, the client may end up feeling more troubled and hopeless in the face of memories that appear to overpower the techniques.

In sum, CBT and EMDR are effective for resolving trauma-related memories to the degree they help clients: a) see these memories as thoughts which interferes with the cycle of maladaptive repetitive thinking associated with these memories and their attendant negative beliefs, emotions, and sensations, and b) allow the default setting of innate mental health/natural trauma resolution to engage.

According to Sydney Banks, sufficient insight regarding the Three Principles is the only intervention necessary—no skills, no techniques, no new beliefs—only sufficient insight regarding the operation of the

Three Principles—particularly the powers of Thought and innate mental health. Even when techniques (e.g., meditation) are used, the change always comes from within and natural healthy feelings appear, such as well-being, gratitude, hope, and love. As such, 3P mental health education is not about helping people change their thoughts; it is about helping them realize that when their thoughts change, their feelings, perceptions, and state of mind also change. Nor is this education meant to help people find techniques or strategies to quiet the mind; it is about helping people realize that when they cease misusing the power of Thought, mental well-being and more positive perceptions of their existing circumstances naturally arise.

A DEEPER DIVE

PODACASTS:

Psychology Has It Backwards, Episode #40—Cognitive Therapies: Better but Still Backwards

Psychology Has It Backwards, Episode #42—Mindfullness: Getting Better

On YouTube watch:

The Difference between the Principles and Cognitive Behavioral Therapy

Natural Mindfulness and the Three Principles: Dicken Bettinger

The Invisible Power and Brilliance of the Human Mind: Ken Manning

CHAPTER 12

Case Examples

Johnny

Johnny, age six, was a happy, outgoing, playful child. His mother, how-ever, was "a worrier." One day Johnny came home from school looking sad. His mother, feeling stressed that day, over-reacted. With an anxious look on her face, she grabbed Johnny's shoulders and queried, "What's wrong? What's wrong?" Johnny—startled by his mother's urgency—started crying. Mom—now more distraught—shouted, "WHAT'S WRONG? —WHAT'S WRONG?" Johnny, really upset at this point, began crying louder. Mom frantically grabbed her phone and called her husband. Their conversation, which Johnny overheard, went something like this,

> "Jim (sobbing)—you've got to come home! I think something bad happened to Johnny. No, he's not hurt. He's horribly upset, and I think that someone at that school might have "bad touched" him or something. No, I can't get him to talk—he won't stop crying. Okay—come home as soon as you can!"

For the rest of the afternoon, Johnny's mother "grilled" him about every minute of his day at school. Johnny kept saying he didn't know why he felt sad. His mother, however, convinced that something bad had happened to Johnny, continued to interrogate him. When Johnny's father arrived, both parents relentlessly questioned him, and soon, Johnny was enrolled in the "something bad happened at school" speculation.

That night Johnny had a nightmare and woke up crying and shaking. His parents rushed to his room and, while nervously comforting him, continued to search for a possible explanation for Johnny's "unusual" behavior. Johnny finally fell asleep, and his parents went back to bed feeling anxious and depressed. The following morning, Johnny awakened complaining of a headache and pleading to stay home from school. A few days later the family met with me.

To make a long story short, nothing bad happened to Johnny. He experienced a discomforting mood—some sad thoughts entered his mind and Johnny felt sad. Startled by his mother's frantic questioning, Johnny began throwing some additional discomforting "thought logs" on the fire. By the time they brought him to see me, Johnny was emersed in anxious thoughts. To cope, he picked what mainstream psychology refers to as "separation anxiety" and a "school phobia."

What started out for Johnny as some sad thoughts—which if left alone would have quickly evaporated—turned into the ingredients of a pernicious misuse of the power of Thought called "worrying." Innocently, Johnny's parents were teaching him to worry.

Ryan

My client, Ryan, complained that it was extremely difficult for him to work with other people. One of Ryan's college professors had divided his class into small groups to work together on term projects. Ryan tried to convince the professor to let him work alone on a term paper. The professor insisted, however, that working in groups was an important class objective. Ryan toyed with withdrawing but needed the class to graduate. So, he asked me to help him figure out why he was "such a loner" and felt so anxious working with others.

I introduced Ryan to the Three Principles, and, during one of our sessions, he recalled an incident from his past that he suspected might relate to his present predicament. Ryan was about nine and walking down the street with his father who suddenly suggested, "Let's race to the corner." Ryan agreed and they started running. About 10 yards from the corner, Ryan's father stuck out his foot and tripped Ryan who took a hard fall. The father completed the race and then sternly admonished his sobbing son, "In this world Ryan, you can't trust anyone!"

Not a very nice thing for a father to do to a son—but bad stuff happens. Anyway, it occurred to Ryan that following this incident, he likely adopted some frightening thoughts about trusting other people. He also recalled that his father was "a loner" and that "both of my parents were very suspicious of other people." It dawned on Ryan that avoiding work with other people was his way of coping with the discomforting feelings spawned by this biased belief. Via grasping sufficient understanding of the Three Principles, however, Ryan was able to recognize these biased thoughts—do his best to not take them to heart—complete his class project—and graduate.

It's helpful to realize that negative thoughts, beliefs, and opinions can only hurt us if—when they happen to mind—we believe them—take them seriously—chronically entertain them! The painful feelings that people experience—and that persist—are created by the discomforting thoughts that people misguidedly think are "the truth" and choose to chronically re-think. We can't stop disordered thoughts from coming to mind. I wish we could, but we can't. We have little say about the thoughts that enter our minds. All kinds of thoughts happen to mind—beautiful thoughts—biased thoughts—stressful thoughts—neutral thoughts. However, we do have a lot to say about these thoughts—once they take form. That's when we encounter the "fork in the road" and our "free will" comes into play. We all have free will to choose what thoughts we honor and invite in for tea and biscuits—and what thoughts we take with "a grain of salt" and allow to pass through. George Pransky put it this way:

"We might have a memory of a childhood trauma or a thought of conscience that we mistreated someone without realizing it. We might feel sadness for the loss of a loved one. All these thoughts are painful, but they would not cause chronic pain because [unless we hold them in mind] they will flow through… and actually be evolved and healed in the process… Chronic stress and distress can only happen in the context of… the thoughts that are deliberately held in mind and re-thought for a period of time."

Meg

Meg saw me for relationship counseling with her boyfriend, Sam. Meg's "issue" was, "I can't trust men!" Meg described several past relationships, stating that in each one, her partner eventually became deceitful and untrustworthy. Sam, she said, was starting to act like all the others.

I asked Meg to recall a time she felt confident she could trust Sam. She reflected for a moment and said, "Well, two weekends ago we spent the night at a romantic bed and breakfast. We had a wonderful time. I remember thinking that night how trustworthy Sam is and how grateful I am to have him in my life. I really trusted him that night!" Before I could comment, however, Meg added that such "trusting times" were becoming less frequent. Sam, she proclaimed, was starting to act in ways that made her very suspicious.

Sam, on the other hand, was at his wit's end. About everything he said or did lately was seen by Meg as either a "put-down" or deceitful. Sam felt "between a rock and a hard place." Even his compliments were typically seen by Meg as insincere.

After observing Meg and Sam interact for one session, I was clear that Meg had picked up a habit of thinking that was obscuring her common sense and distorting her view of Sam's actions. When this thinking "kicked in," Meg innocently misperceived and over-reacted to many of Sam's innocuous statements, gestures, and behaviors. Meg's biased personal thoughts were creating views of Sam's behaviors that looked real to her—but weren't. Unless Meg gained a sufficient understanding of the

Three Principles that allowed her to recognize and discount these biased thoughts, she would never meet a man she would trust for very long.

Frank

Frank, was "a neat freak." Unless everything in his car, home, and office was exactly "in place," Frank felt anxious and insecure. Frank demanded the same orderly behavior from his girlfriend who eventually got fed up with his nagging and threatened to leave him if he didn't "back off" and get some help.

During one of our sessions, Frank recalled an incident from his past that he thought might relate to his "obsession with order." Frank was five and playing in the family room with his older brothers, ages seven and nine. Frank's mother told the boys to stop playing and clean up the room. When their mother returned and found the boys still "horsing around" she over-reacted and screamed something like, "If you boys don't get this room spotless right now, I'm going to leave, and you won't have a mother." The brothers immediately straightened up the room.

That night, Frank's nine-year-old brother got up to use the bathroom and found little Frank sitting in the bathtub trying to clean it! He quickly awakened their mother and led her to the bathroom. She plucked Frank up from the tub—told him he didn't have to clean it—tucked him back in bed.

It occurred to Frank that he may have made this event mean that his security and well-being depended on making sure everything was neat and clean. He also recalled that his mother had "a thing about neatness"—that her favorite saying was, "Cleanliness is next to Godliness." Frank realized that when "things appeared to be out of order" he felt guilty and anxious. He also realized that this compulsive behavior temporarily relieved these uncomfortable feelings. Through a sufficient understanding of the Three Principles, Frank saw the vicious cycle in which he was innocently trapped. He also realized that his anxious feelings were "his friends" trying to warn him that his thinking was off kilter. With these new insights, Frank was finally able to shed his "neat freak" reputation.

Liz

Liz, a 23-year-old college student, was sitting at her desk on day one of her American History class. Her professor arrived a few minutes late—a tall, slender man, about 60 or so, with a long, white beard. Upon making eye contact with the professor, Liz's heart began to pound, and her hands started shaking. She became so uncomfortable she got up and left the classroom! Liz tried to calm down in a nearby lounge. A few minutes later she attempted to re-enter the classroom. However, as she glanced at the professor through the window in the classroom door, her panicky feelings flared up. Feeling "shook up" and confused, Liz decided to consult with me to find out what was going on.

After assuring Liz that her mental health was fine, I introduced her to the Three Principles and described the inextricable connection between people's thoughts and their experiences. I suggested to Liz that some painful memories may have come to mind. At our next session, Liz shared the following incident from her past that her mother had recalled. Liz was about four—riding her tricycle on the sidewalk near her home. She hit a bump—lost her balance—fell off her trike—hit her head on the sidewalk. A man walking on the other side of the street ran across to see if Liz was okay. Liz's mother also saw Liz fall and came running toward her at about the same time. Little Liz—bruised, frightened, and dazed from the fall—looked up at the Good Samaritan bending over her and panicked. She struggled to her feet and ran, sobbing and shaking into her mother's arms. Her mother described the stranger as an older man, very tall and thin—with a long white beard!

Bud

Bud, a university colleague, asked my opinion about an incident that he couldn't fully understand. Bud was researching juvenile gangs in Detroit and had interviewed a 14-year-old boy who was a member of a violent youth gang. For some reason, after the interview, Bud asked the boy if he had ever seen the Detroit Zoo. When the boy said "No," Bud invited him to join his family the following Sunday to check out the Zoo. To Bud's surprise, the boy accepted his invitation!

The following Sunday, Bud, his wife, and their two young children met the boy at a fast-food restaurant near his neighborhood. According to Bud, "During the drive to the Zoo, the boy was immersed in his "tough guy" image. You could see it in his demeanor, his voice, and his language. It was quite disturbing to all of us. I thought I'd made a big mistake!"

It was after they arrived at the Zoo that the situation occurred that Bud couldn't fully understand. According to Bud, "It was like magic! This tough, gangster-like kid transformed into a typical 14-year-old adolescent! His voice changed from 'deep macho' to an easy, natural tone. His gate shifted from an exaggerated 'swagger' to a normal stride. His body relaxed and his stern grimace faded. He began smiling and interacting affectionately with my children. The kid transformed from Mr. Hyde to Dr. Jekyll!"

Bud reported that the metamorphosis lasted most of the afternoon. However, during the drive home, through the rearview mirror, Bud saw the boy slowly shift back to his gangster persona. As he exited the car with a swagger and a "thumbs up" gesture of "thanks," the reverse transformation was complete. Mr. Hyde was back!

Bud's story is a poignant example of the innate health that lies beneath the conditioned thoughts of even the most chronic, hard-core juvenile offenders. When this youth was away from his neighborhood—accompanied by a caring, non-judgmental family—absorbed in a unique experience—his personal mind quieted—he forgot "who he thought he was"—and his innate health and "true self" surfaced.

Sally

Sally, age 19, was a highly ranked competitive figure skater. She was referred to me by her mother because she was practicing 9-10 hours a day and neglecting her family, college classes, and friends. I asked Sally, "How many hours a day do you need to practice to maintain your competitive edge?" She responded, "Maybe five or six." Then I asked her, "Why are you practicing an extra 4 to 5 hours every day?" Sally quickly replied, "I love to practice!"

Later, it became clear that when Sally wasn't practicing, she was a chronic worrier and perfectionist. Practicing was her excuse to quiet her mind and fall into the present moment. However, not realizing that the source of her well-being was her own innate health, Sally was addicted to practicing. However, when Sally grasped a sufficient understanding of the Three Principles, she realized that she could bring the same healthy experience that bubbled up during her practice sessions into the rest of her life.

A Case from Michael Neill, Author of "The Inside-Out Revolution

I once worked with a young woman who had been diagnosed with obsessive-compulsive disorder (OCD), which manifested in her repeatedly returning home from work during the day to check that her front door was locked, and all her appliances were safely unplugged or switched off. It had gotten to the point where she was given a leave of absence from her job. On the one hand, they didn't want to lose her; on the other hand, she sometimes wouldn't make it into the office until after 11am, having gone back and forth on the bus multiple times.

When we got together, she recounted her story and her desire to "get herself under control." I spoke with her about the creative nature of Thought and Consciousness and how they worked together like a virtual reality simulator to make everything we think seem real to us. I also pointed her towards her own common sense and the real-time responsive intelligence of the deeper mind.

After a time, she settled down and asked me a question. "Why aren't you telling me to stop?" When I asked her what she meant, she said

"Everybody I've talked with about this has tried to get me to stop imagining crazy things and to just tough it out. You haven't even mentioned what you think I should do." "That seems like it would be a really mean thing to do," I replied. "After all, if you were on the bus to work and you saw a child with a puppy in the lobby of a burning building, wouldn't you leap off the bus and try to rescue them?" She thought about it for a few moments and then said that she'd like to think that she would. "Me too," I continued. "So, if I tried to stop you from doing that, wouldn't that be horrible of me?"

She looked confused but thoughtful. "So, are you saying that I'm not insane to keep going home to check on my apartment?" "As long as it looks to you like you really did leave your apartment unlocked with all the appliances running, it would be insane NOT to go home and take care of it. But if you start to see how the power of Thought is creating your reality, you'll notice that some things stop looking quite so real to you. And when it doesn't really look like your home is at risk, you won't be inclined to leave work to go check on it."

We went on to have a conversation about how once you get eyes for it, it's pretty easy to get a feel for what's coming to us via the arbitrary randomness of our personal thinking and what's coming to us via our inner knowing. By this point, we were both pretty quiet, and I had a sense that she'd heard something fundamental enough to change the game going forward. The next time I heard from her, she was back at work and doing well. "I still go back to double-check the apartment from time to time," she said as though in a mischievous confessional. "But it doesn't bother me anymore because I know it doesn't mean anything bad about me— just that from time to time I have some pretty nutty thinking. And like you said to me when we first spoke, 'If you're nuts but you know that you're nuts, you're not that nuts.'"

Since that time, I've come to see the truth of what Syd Banks shared with the inmates. We really are doing the best we can given the thinking we have that looks real to us. Or, to put it another way: If I'm operating in a world where people are out to get me and have the power to take away my happiness, common sense tells me I need to protect myself from them. Depending on how I've learned to cope with the world, I might attempt to do that by cutting them out of my life, by hurting them before they hurt me, or by trying to minimize the risk by doing whatever they want me to do, no matter how arbitrary or unpleasant it seems. Each one of these behaviors makes perfect sense *given the fundamental premise that people are out to get me*. But if we look towards a more universal truth, we see that well-being is innate, people's motivations are the fruits of their often random or habitual thinking, and we're not as separate from one another as we think. And when we look past our nutty premises towards a deeper, more fundamental truth, we begin to walk in a different world. The same common sense that led us to protect ourselves in whatever way we thought best will now guide us to follow the inner wisdom and unfolding of the energy and intelligence behind life.

The Author

Another misguided way that most of us learned to misuse the power of Thought is *egotistical thinking*—using the power of Thought to create an "ego" or "self-image"—the illusion that our self-worth is tied to external factors such as our attributes (e.g., looks, intelligence)—accomplishments (e.g., awards, money)—circumstances (e.g., being promoted, being fired)—and how other people treat us (e.g., bullying). This common misuse of the power of Thought is grounded in the misguided idea that one's worth or value must be earned. Here's how it works. People select their "self-worth items" from their cultural menu. Then, they work like crazy to check these items off the list. Soon, they find themselves trapped in a never-ending spiral of self-consciousness, self-monitoring, and self-evaluation. Perform, assess, rate yourself—perform, assess, judge yourself—assess, judge, measure your worth. When people meet their self-worth standards, they experience arrogance and pride—an "ego-high." When they fall short of their self-worth expectations, they experience self-doubt and insecurity—an "ego-low." Doesn't sound very peaceful and serene—does it?

I began creating this health-obscuring Thought misuse early on. When I was about two and a half, my mother, father, and grandfather spent hours reading poems to me from a Mother Goose book of nursery rhymes. The book had drawings that illustrated classic poems like, "The Owl and the Pussy Cat," "How Would You like to go up in a Swing," "I Eat My Peas with Honey," and "The Night before Christmas." My family read these poems to me perhaps hundreds of times.

One day, I asked my grandfather if I could read some poems to him. "Papa" agreed and, as my mother remembered it, "He nearly fainted!" Apparently, I recited most of the poems in the book—almost word for word—turning the pages at the right time. I couldn't read and I wasn't trying to prove anything. I had memorized the poems—a natural outcome of being fully immersed in the moment.

Here's what followed, however. My father, Larry Kelley, was an announcer at WXYZ Radio in Detroit. He helped produce several classic radio shows including "The Lone Ranger" and "The Green Hornet." He taped me talking with him and reciting some of the poems and presented the tape to his station manager. A few weeks later, "The Little Tommy Kelley Show" aired coast-to-coast on the Mutual Broadcasting Network.

I don't remember any of this. However, my mother said that the show was written up in several local and national magazines and newspapers, and I received loads of letters and postcards from listeners. I was labeled a "child prodigy" and received loads of attention—*tied to my performance on the show.* That's likely when my ego began to take form. Initially, memorizing and reciting poems is something that many young children do naturally and effortlessly. I suspect, however, that I misguidedly began to think—*and believe*—that my worth was tied to being seen by others as "special."

Over time, my egotistical thoughts grew from a trickle to a torrent. By the time I started school, I'd created a nice-sized little ego. I thought that I had to get all A's to be "good enough." I experienced loads of anxiety during my school years. If I thought a teacher was upset with me, I couldn't sleep. I coped by over-preparing for tests—reading each chapter four or five times—cheating, if necessary, to stay on top.

On Friday afternoon—following a perfect exam score—I might allow my personal mind to relax a bit. For a while, I would feel more at ease and spontaneous. It wouldn't be long, however, before my "ego thoughts" would kick back in. Then, I would start feeling anxious and off I'd go—upstairs to my room to study. In her book, "The Path to Contentment," Elsie Spittle talks about "being ordinary:"

> "One of the things Syd often spoke about was being ordinary. I'd been ordinary all my life, so I wasn't enamored with his direction to 'be ordinary.' He would tell us that once we'd had an insight, to just live, be ordinary, and go about our everyday business. He told us we'd see the world differently; that our many 'issues' would become non-issues, that we'd have far more enjoyment with the simple things in life. I found this a bit perturbing. It's true that my life had indeed changed a great deal, but I was hanging on to the need to feel special, not ordinary. The feeling was subtle; so subtle I didn't see it for a while. Misinterpreting and confusing the Principles' message of hope and transformation with my ego's desire to be something special in this world soon brought me to the realization that being special was an ever-elusive goal. The longer I hung on to that need, the less special I felt. My life once again felt like it was in a tailspin. Go figure!"

Bob

Bob was required to attend therapy as a condition of his parole. One of the first things Bob wanted to discuss with me was an experience he had in prison that puzzled him. Bob was assigned to clean the prison's latrines. At first, he was outraged, thinking, "I always get the short straw!" However, Bob decided to carry out this assignment the best he could. After a few days on the job, he began looking forward to his time in the bathrooms. He said he often felt joyful while he worked and had helpful new insights about his life. Bob exclaimed, "Every morning I couldn't wait to start cleaning those toilets!" After a few months, however, Bob had another thought, "I must be crazy to love this work!" The thought that followed was more perplexing, "Janitorial work must be my true calling in life."

I assisted Bob to understand the Three Principles, the power of Thought, and the power of innate mental health. Bob realized that the exhilaration he experienced in prison wasn't caused by cleaning the latrines. Rather, he saw that the source of his exhilaration was his own innate mental health bubbling-up while he was absorbed in his work and "thinking at the speed of life." Bob realized that he didn't have to be a janitor to access this health. He lightened up and eventually enrolled in an auto mechanics training program.

Darla

Darla lost her home and most of her Florida neighborhood courtesy of hurricane Katrina. At our first session, she reported feeling depressed and guilty because, "I felt happier and more alive after Katrina hit than ever before!" For several weeks following the storm, Darla immersed herself in the rescue and clean-up operations. When these activities quieted down, however, Darla reverted to her old habits of worry and self-abasement. Following Three Principles education, however, Darla realized that the source of her exhilaration following Katrina was her own innate health. She also realized that she could access this health on her own rather than wait for another hurricane.

A DEEPER DIVE

On YouTube watch:

Stories of Hope: Bill Pettit

Girl Freed from Anxiety: Dicken Bettinger

Thought Has No Power with Judy Sedgeman

Book:

Modello: A Story of Hope for the Inner-City and Beyond by Jack Pransky

PART VI

Applications & Research

Considerable preliminary research offers support for the efficacy of mental health education grounded in the Three Principles understanding for improving the mental health, physical health, and behavior of people in a variety of settings (publications regarding these applications and research are listed in Appendix 1). In the three chapters that follow, Three Principles applications are described for people in prison for sexual violence, school failure and delinquency, and physical ill-health.

CHAPTER 13

People in Prison for Sexual Violence

The Problem

Sexual violence (or SV) remains a serious mental health and social problem. Data from the National Intimate Partner and Sexual Violence Survey shows that during their lifetime, approximately 1 in 5 women in the United States have experienced rape or attempted rape, and 43.9% have experienced other forms of SV. For instance, 12.5% have experienced sexual coercion, 27.3% unwanted sexual contact, and 32.1% non-contact unwanted sexual experiences. Men are also impacted by SV. During their lifetime, approximately 1 in 15 men (6.7%) have been forced to penetrate someone, 5.8% have experienced sexual coercion, 10.8% unwanted sexual contact, and 13.3% non-contact unwanted sexual experiences. Children are also victims of SV, with an estimated 1 in 6 boys and 1 in 4 girls experiencing some form of sexual abuse before age 18.

For England and Wales, findings from the National Crime Recording Standard (NCRS) show the highest SV figure recorded by the police and the largest annual percentage increase in SV since the introduction of the NCRS in April 2002! The NCRS showed 88,106 police recorded sexual offences in the year ending in March 2016, an increase of 37% compared with the previous year. Within the overall increase, the number of offences of rape increased by 41%, and the number of other sexual offences increased by 35%. While these increases are believed to have resulted in large part from both an improvement in the recording of sexual offences by the police, and an increased willingness of victims to report these crimes to the police, they are striking, nevertheless.

Mainstream Psychology's View

In response to these and other forms of SV and their often-damaging psychological impact on many victims, perpetrators, families, and society, effective treatment for sex offenders remains a pressing issue in the U.S. and the U.K. Over the past decade, there has been a substantial increase in empirical research regarding the efficacy of interventions designed to prevent SV and reduce its recurrence. The consensus of several meta-analytic studies regarding best treatment practices for juvenile and adult offenders is that CBT is more effective for reducing sexual recidivism than other interventions (e.g., general psychotherapy, behavioral reconditioning, pharmacological interventions, criminal sanctions). On average, however, compared to people not treated, the reduction in sexual and other forms of recidivism achieved by CBT-based interventions is typically small. For example, a highly respected meta-analysis assessed the effectiveness of offender treatment and included 69 controlled studies involving 22,181 participants. Based on an average follow-up period of slightly more than 5 years, the researchers found an average sexual recidivism rate of 11.1 percent for offenders treated using CBT compared with 17.5 percent recidivism for untreated offenders! Additional meta-analyses reported that treated offenders showed a 12 percent reduction in recidivism compared to a 22 percent reduction in recidivism for offenders not treated! Following a narrative review of offender treatment effectiveness studies, the authors concluded, "…the most reasonable estimate at this point is that treatment can reduce sexual recidivism over a 5-year period by 5-8%."

The Three Principles' View

The major reason for the limited impact of CBT-based (and other) interventions for people prone to sexual violence is that these interventions are not grounded in the Three Principles that explain the way people's psychological experiences and behavior are created. Absent recognition and direction of Principles, the effectiveness of CBT-based (and other) interventions will continue to bear small fruit.

Gauging One's Propensity for SV

In his book, *Prevention from the Inside-Out*, Jack Pransky envisioned the following formula to gauge people's propensity for SV:

$$\text{Propensity for SV} = \frac{\text{Personal Norm + Habit + Arousal}}{\text{Understanding + Perspective + Wisdom}}$$

The factors in the formula's numerator combine to create SV: a) *Personal Norm* – the degree to which a person believes SV is acceptable; b) *Habit* – the degree to which SV is a person's habitual response; and c) *Arousal* – the extent of a person's desire or impulse, *in the moment,* to engage in SV. Personal norm can place people on the path toward SV. The extent to which people believe SV is an acceptable action determines their propensity to engage in SV. Habit can start people down the path to SV. Arousal can often propel people down the road. What these three factors have in common is that SV-prone people misguidedly view each factor as "the truth" rather than an experience they have created with their own personal thinking which, when enlivened via consciousness, looks and feels real to them, which is what makes them act.

Regarding each of these factors, people's understanding and perspective, in the moment, can be at numerous levels. For example, if a person believes SV is acceptable, does not want to stop, and is highly aroused in the moment, they will likely perpetrate SV. On the other hand, if the person believes that SV is unthinkable and has no propensity to engage in SV—for instance, if aroused, their habit may be to simply masturbate instead, causing no harm to others—and is experiencing wellbeing in the moment, it would be unlikely for them to perpetrate SV. A wide range of degrees of perspective and understanding exist between these two poles.

The following examples, best read from the bottom up, represent higher ascending levels of in-the-moment understanding and perspective:

Personal Norm about SV: The "Reality" One Generally Believes about SV:

- SV is horrible. Under no circumstances is it acceptable.
- SV is not good.
- SV is not okay, but I slip sometimes.
- Something doesn't feel right about SV, but. . .
- SV is the way to be and to act.

Habit of SV: The "Reality" One Is Inclined to Act Upon and the "Stops" One Puts on Themself:

- SV is out of the question for me. I can't even imagine it.
- I am absolutely committed to stopping.
- This is not right, and I really, deeply would like to stop.
- I'm nervous about doing this bad thing and I would like to stop.
- Something about it doesn't feel quite right, and I'd kind of like to stop, but I can't help myself.
- I have no desire to stop committing SV.

Arousal: The Compelling, Exciting Feeling or Urge in a Moment to Have Sexual Release and/or to Exert Power/Control over Someone Perceived to Be Weaker:

- Love and peace—Great love for all; harming others is inconceivable; we're all connected as one.

- Compassion—If I take advantage of someone, that person will be hurt. It is not good or right.
- Neutral—No feeling; not aroused at all.
- Attraction—I appreciate how this person looks or their energy.
- Twinge—I feel a tiny pull toward wanting this person.
- Desire—I want this person.
- Compelled—I feel pulled to go after this person.
- Driven—I must go after this person, no choice.

The three factors in the formula's denominator combine to prevent SV: a) *Understanding*—the degree to which people prone to SV realize that the source of each factor in the numerator is their own thinking made to look and feel real via consciousness; b) *Perspective*—the extent to which these individuals realize this (i.e., are able to access this understanding) *in the moment;* and c) *Wisdom*—extent to which these people listen to and are guided by their own common sense or internal awareness of what is appropriate. The level of understanding and perspective in the moment, regarding each factor in the numerator, plus the ability to realize and trust their innate wisdom, can divert these individuals from the path to SV.

In sum, to help people change from a proclivity toward SV, they need to understand that the source of the three factors that underlie SV is their *own thinking* and to realize how each of these factors is altered by how their thinking makes it appear. The extent to which SV-prone people realize *in the moment* that each factor in the numerator is formed via their own thoughts made to look real via consciousness; the more likely they are to access the wisdom necessary to eclipse their habitual behavior and avoid SV.

This is what has been missing in CBT and other methods to reduce the incidence and prevalence of SV. No matter what skills and techniques are mastered by people prone to SV, the way these people view a situation and/or a potential victim in general, plus the understanding and perspective they have *in the moment* is what will determine their likelihood at any given time of engaging in SV. *Put another way, even if the factors in the numerator exist, the degree to which a potential SV perpetrator has understanding and perspective in the moment that what they are experiencing is not reality, but only their own thoughts producing one of numerous possible realities will determine whether they engage in SV.* No matter what thoughts people have about norm, habit, and arousal, if they gain a sufficient understanding of the "inside-out" evolution of everyone's psychological experiences and have perspective, in the moment, to access this understanding, the level of all three factors in the numerator will decrease and the likelihood of SV will descend.

Supportive Research

Jacqueline Hollows, Jack Pransky, Alena Kryvanos, Sarah Bowen, and I conducted a study that examined the efficacy of Three Principles mental health education for improving the mental health and self-control of people in prison for sexual violence. Our study was published in *Violence Against Women* (Kelley, Hollows, Pransky, Kryvanos, & Bowen, 2021). A summary of this study follows:

The Participants

The location is HM Prison Rye Hill in Willoughby, Warwickshire, United Kingdom (UK). Case managers at the Prison referred 132 residents as potential candidates for the intervention. Of these residents, 67 completed the intervention and formed the treatment group. The remaining 65 residents decided not to enroll and formed the control group. The offenses committed by participants included rape of adult women, rape of children and babies, molestation, and gang sexual crimes. Some participants were also convicted of additional crimes such as drug dealing, drug importation, robbery, and assault. The two groups did not differ significantly on age, ethnicity, or education.

Sentence length for participants ranged from 4 years to life, with some participants serving consecutive sentences. There were no significant differences between the treatment and control participants on offense type or sentence length.

The Intervention

Ten 3-day intensive 3P classes were facilitated by two 3P practitioners, each with 4-6 years of experience teaching the Three Principles to people under criminal justice system supervision. The 3P intervention contained the following modules: building rapport; exploration of "reality;" separate realities; exploration of thought, insight, and consciousness—where do they come from; exploring feelings/moods/behavior; exploring innate health/natural intelligence; what is Mind; exploring infinite potential; exploring mental clarity versus a busy mind; stepping into the unknown; implications of the Three Principles for prison life; and living outside of prison.

The program format allowed flexibility for the facilitators to trust their own wisdom to guide each session. Sessions were exploratory and reflective rather than traditional lecturing/teaching. Conversations were often based on what participants brought into the room and the facilitators continually looked for opportunities to teach the thought-experience connection and highlight each participant's innate health/wisdom.

The Results

Pre-and post-intervention, participants completed the Three Principles Inventory, Warwick-Edinburgh Mental Well-Being Survey, Grasmick Low Self-Control Scale, and the PROMIS-Short Form depression, anxiety, and anger scales. Compared with the control group, participants receiving 3P education showed a significant increase in mental wellbeing, a significant reduction in depression, anxiety, and anger, and a significant increase in self-control.

A DEEPER DIVE

On YouTube watch:

3PGC – Freedom Exists Within the Prison of Our Mind with Jacqueline Hollows

The Three Principles: Bringing Hope into Prisons and Drug & Alcohol Rehabilitation

I've Gotten Impacted by the Three Principles: Now What? Cathy Casey

Group Discussion: Anger and Resentment

3GPC Anger and Taking Things Personally

3PGC From Gang Member to Military Uniformity to Light and Love – My Secret Interview with Rob Cook

CHAPTER 14

School Failure and Delinquency

The Problem

Mental well-being and positive perceptions of school climate (or SC) are particularly important for students at risk for school failure and delinquency. Regarding SC, considerable research shows that students at risk who report positive perceptions of their SC are less likely to be overcome by negative influences and risk factors that can impede academic success and promote drop-out and other problem behaviors. Several independent reviews of SC research conclude that positive perceptions of SC by students at risk are associated with several beneficial outcomes, including improved academic achievement and graduation rates and decreased delinquency, drug use, truancy, and drop-out. Furthermore, students at risk who report positive perceptions of their SC have fewer discipline referrals, fewer harassment events and bullying incidents, fewer suspensions and expulsions, less fighting and antisocial behavior, higher attendance and graduation rates, and heightened relational trust with school peers, school staff, and parents. Positive perceptions of SC by students at risk can also reduce achievement gaps among students of different socioeconomic backgrounds and between students with stronger and weaker academic abilities.

Considerable research also shows that perceptions of SC for students at risk are tightly intertwined with their mental well-being. The consensus of this research is students who report positive perceptions of their SC also report higher levels of mental well-being, self-efficacy, resilience, creativity, satisfaction, and hope for the future. Furthermore, positive views of SC by students at risk are consistently associated with lower levels of mental stress, depression, and anxiety.

Mainstream Psychology's View

The robust positive relationship between SC perceptions and mental well-being for students at risk is well-documented. However, the direction of this relationship remains unclear. Mainstream psychology's prevailing view is that the well-being of students at risk is significantly affected by the climate at their schools. This view has spawned a plethora of packages, programs, therapies, and techniques designed to "build" or construct more positive SCs from the "outside-in."

The Three Principles' View

Instead of students' mental health being affected by their school climate, students with poor mental health typically have more negative perceptions of their school climate. Put another way, students with good mental health typically have more positive perceptions of their SC. This "inside-out" view posits that if the mental health of students at risk improves, their perceptions of their SC will also improve *without changing anything external at their school.*

Students at risk for school failure and delinquency do not often realize the distinction between what is happening in the outside world and their experience of it—the meaning they make of it with their own thinking. These students do not typically recognize that their own thoughts are the source of their psychological experiences. Rather, these students often confuse the source of their experiences with what is happening "out there"— within outside reality. A student's anger is coming from a fellow student, a teacher, a parent. The very next day, however, the same student might respond differently to the very same people, because their thoughts have changed.

Students at risk can be assisted to recognize, in the moment, that what they experience is their own thoughts made to appear real via their consciousness. If these students do not realize this fact, they will typically take their personal thoughts to heart and often act on whatever "reality" these thoughts create. On the other hand, if these students realize what they are doing, they will be less likely to view these thoughts as "the truth" or the way things really are.

Furthermore, students at risk do not often realize the tremendous resource of innate mental health that is readily available to them. These students tend to obscure this health via innocently misusing the power of Thought. However, they can be assisted to notice what they experience when they fall into the present moment (e.g., are lost or absorbed in some activity). They can be assisted to recognize that mental well-being is always available to them and that only their own personal thoughts can obscure this health. Finally, students at risk do not often realize they have an internal gauge that will reliably inform them when their thinking is off—their feelings. This means that by using the signal of a negative or discomforting feeling, these students can discount their personal thoughts and allow their innate well-being to surface.

Supportive Research

Brooke Wheeldon-Reece, Eric Lambert, and I conducted a study that investigated the efficacy of Three Principles mental health education for improving the mental health and perceptions of school climate for students at risk for school failure (or students at risk). Our study was published in the *Journal of Spiritual Psychology and Counselling* (Kelley, Wheeldon Reece, & Lambert, 2021). A summary of this study follows:

The Participants

Five schools in lower-income neighborhoods in Hillsborough County, Florida, agreed to participate. Administrators at each school informed their students and caregivers of the availability of this intervention, emphasizing that participation was voluntary. One hundred nine students agreed to participate. All participants were identified by their schools as at-risk for academic failure based on failing grades, overdue and incomplete homework assignments, truancy, and disruptive classroom behaviors (e.g., profanity, fighting). Participants' grade levels ranged from 8 through 12. Participants' ages ranged from 12 to 19 years with a mean age of 14.81 years. 68% reported as female and 32% as male. Approximately 86% reported as Black or Latinx, and 14% as White. A treatment group of 75 students and a waitlist control group of 34 students were formed.

The Intervention

Three Principles mental health education was facilitated by two instructors each with several years of experience teaching the Three Principles understanding to middle school and high school students. Classes met weekly for 45-60 minutes during regular school hours for 13 consecutive weeks. Each class contained between 7 and 17 students. The average attendance was 87% or approximately 11.5 of the 13 sessions. All 75 treatment participants completed at least seven classes.

The curriculum contained the following core lessons: overview and introduction; the Principles behind your life; the power of Thought; your personal guide to decision making; community engagement; how state of mind influences judgment and reasoning; surviving mood swings; finding success amid stress, feeling fear and insecurity without fear and insecurity; the inside-out nature of self-esteem; separate realities; cultivating meaningful relationships; dating and healthy relationships; mentoring and leading from the inside-out; bully prevention from the inside-out; academic success; college and career readiness; financial stability; parenting from the inside-out; creating the life designed for you; and graduation.

In the 3P-based classes, stories, metaphors, symbols, videos, group activities, discussions, and games are used to introduce participants to the Principles of Universal Mind, Consciousness, and Thought and to help students grasp the way these Principles manifest within everyone. For example, the metaphor of the sun and clouds was used to represent how a student's innate health (i.e., the sun) can become obscured by their personal thoughts (i.e., the clouds) and, like the sun, this health is always there. Also, the metaphor of a tea bag being converted into tea by hot water was used to illustrate how thoughts are made to appear real via consciousness. 3P instructors also assisted students to recognize that mental health does not mean that people feel good all the time; that people's feelings, perceptions, and states of mind change as their thinking changes. Students are further assisted to realize that the sensory manifestations of their thinking cannot damage or hurt them no matter how extreme, painful, or insecure they feel.

The Results

Compared with the control group, students exposed to Three Principles mental health education showed improved mental health evidenced by a significant increase in wellbeing, state of mind, and hope for the future. They also showed improved perceptions of school climate evidenced by a significant increase in communication and conflict resolution, valuing academic success, and relational trust with school peers, school staff, and parents.

Implications for the School Community

There is substantial evidence from several decades of research that mental well-being and positive perceptions of school climate are routinely associated with improved academic achievement and heightened social and emotional development of students, particularly students at risk for school failure and other health-damaging behaviors. However, absent sufficient recognition that Thought is the formulator of people's every psychological experience, schools continue to focus on external strategies to improve the well-being and school climate perceptions of students at risk. These "outside-in" approaches may temporarily help quiet the minds of some students and release their innate well-being. However, "renting" improved well-being pales in comparison to "owning" this health via realizing the way the Principles of Universal Mind, Consciousness, and Thought manifest within everyone to create their psychological experiences.

When students (and other school community members) are exposed to mental health education grounded in the Three Principles and, in turn, grasp a sufficient insight-based understanding of the power of Thought and the power of innate mental health, their mental well-being and school climate perceptions naturally improve. Students begin learning with more spontaneity and creativity via an enhanced capacity for insight. Students and teachers become more receptive to change and feel less compelled to defend their ingrained beliefs. Teachers take the negative states of mind of their students less personally. Students' minds relax and the grip of their typical or habitual personal thinking begins to loosen, so they are more open to new perspectives. Judy Sedgeman stated:

> "Once people understand the thought-experience connection and realize how to re-access a healthy state of mind, they can sustain day-to-day peace of mind, wisdom, and well-being regardless of circumstances."

A DEEPER DIVE

On YouTube watch:

3PGC – Bringing the Principles into Prevention and Education with Brooke Wheeldon-Reece

Educating Children about 3 Principles In (& Out of) School

Managing Stress for Students and Teens: Ann Curtis

CHAPTER 15

Physical Ill-Health:
Chronic Fatigue & Eating Disorders

The Problem

Chronic Fatigue Syndrome (or CFS), also known as Myalgic Encephalo-myelitis (or ME), is typically a long-term illness with a variety of medical symptoms, including severe and often disabling fatigue, headaches, sleep disturbances, depression, anxiety, difficulties with attention and concentration, and muscle pain. The severity of CFS varies between cases and within cases over time. In the worst cases, people are bedridden or wheelchair bound. While CFS affects children, it typically develops in adults between their mid-20's and mid-40's. The etiology of CFS has not been fully determined. Thus, CFS is typically diagnosed following the exclusion of other possible illnesses.

Epidemiological estimates of the prevalence of CFS vary between 0.5 and 2.5% of the general population. In the U.S. around one million people meet the criteria for CFS. In the U.K., the Department of Health Working Party on CFS estimated that a typical general practice physician has 40 patients with CFS. Because of its high prevalence and related physical and psychological disabilities, CFS is associated with high direct and indirect costs for contemporary health care and society.

Mainstream Psychology's View

In absence of causative therapies, mainstream psychology uses a variety of modalities to treat CFS, including pharmacological, nutritional, immunological, exercise, and psychological. At present, the two most used psychological interventions are CBT and graded exercise treatment (or GET). Findings of randomized controlled studies show low to moderate short-term effects for CBT and GET, and mixed conclusions for the long-term effects of both modalities. Furthermore, CBT and GET may be unsuitable for certain people with CFS, such as those so severely ill they are unable to exercise or practice CBT techniques. In sum, the effectiveness of CBT and GET compared to support groups, natural course, and standard medical care appears to be moderate at best and typically falls far short of full recovery.

A recent development in treating CFS is the addition of mindfulness-based interventions (or MBIs) to the standard rehabilitation approach. Early research shows that MBIs appear to reduce levels of fatigue and improve mood, physical functioning, and quality of life. However, additional research is needed to determine the efficacy of MBIs.

The Three Principles' View

Viewed through the logic of the Three Principles, individuals diagnosed with CFS have several misunderstandings about their illness and their psychological functioning that causes them to live in chronic stressful thinking and the chronic mental stress it spawns. Below are three examples:

Misunderstanding 1: Health/wellbeing results from eliminating symptoms and achieving specific goals.

Output of This Misunderstanding: Chronic overthinking about physical symptoms, personal circumstances, and treatment goals results in chronic mental stress, obscures innate health/wellbeing, and creates further symptoms.

3P Education: Health/wellbeing is not dependent on circumstances and goal attainment. Rather, this health is available to people before they get lost in chronic overthinking regarding their circumstances, symptoms, and goals.

Misunderstanding 2: It is up to the individual to manage their energy and symptoms by constantly thinking about them and continually monitoring their actions.

Output of This Misunderstanding: An increasing tendency to focus on symptoms and their management. Over time, this results in apprehension regarding normal somatic sensations and restrictions of movement which, in turn, sets the stage for further deterioration.

3P Education: The body is not managed by one's thinking. The body is managed by the intelligence of Universal Mind. If an intervention regarding one's symptoms makes sense, this awareness or "knowingness" will come to the person via Universal Mind, not from chronic over-thinking and monitoring of one's feelings and symptoms.

Misunderstanding 3: People's thinking provides an objective and useful projection of their future circumstances.

Output of This Misunderstanding: When individuals have anxious thoughts about their symptoms or their lives, they tend to believe these thoughts and try to figure out how to avoid or resolve them. This results in further stimulation of the fight/flight response and exacerbation of their symptoms.

3P Education: One's personal thoughts are subjective, ebb and flow, and are transient. These thoughts cannot be relied upon to accurately predict the future and they can change one's perspective quickly. People can better react to the unknown in real-time by trusting their innate health/ wisdom to guide them.

Three Principles education attempts to help these individuals grasp new insights regarding the power of Thought and the power of innate mental health that can help correct these misunderstandings, "short-circuit" their maladaptive habits of personal thinking, and allow their body's nervous system to calm down.

Supportive Research

John El-Mokadem, Karen DiMarko, Laura Duffield, and I conducted a study that investigated the efficacy of Three Principles mental health education for people diagnosed with chronic fatigue syndrome. Our study was published in the American Psychological Association-sponsored journal, *Spirituality in Clinical Practice* (El-Mokadem, DiMarko, Kelley, & Duffield, 2020). A summary of our study follows:

The Participants

Twenty-two adults diagnosed with CFS participated. Using a random list generator, participants were assigned to a treatment group (n = 11) and a waitlist control group (n = 11). Among the 22 participants, 19 reported as female and three reported as male. Participants' ages ranged from 19 to 66 years, with a mean age of 42.9. Regarding country of origin, for the treatment group, seven were from the U.K., three from the U.S., and one from Ireland. For the control group, eight were from the U.K., one from Norway, one from New Zealand, and one from Slovakia. The 3P intervention was facilitated by two 3P mental health educators each with several years of experience teaching the Three Principles. The intervention was eight weeks in duration and contained the following components:

Weekly Educational Videos & Reading Assignments

Participants viewed weekly educational videos narrated by the 3P facilitators and completed assigned 3P-based readings. The first video described the mind/body link, the relationship between CFS symptoms and chronic mental stress, and the value for healing via recognizing and discounting one's personal thoughts and freeing up the body's innate intelligence/resilience. Examples of other topics addressed in the videos are: why re-thinking stressful thoughts regarding CFS symptoms sustains these symptoms and confirms the illusion of a prolonged and serious illness; how the mind is built to settle and why people don't need to fear painful/insecure feelings; how attending to stressful thoughts about a potential relapse stirs up the stress response and creates symptoms that confirm the perception that a relapse is inevitable and an insidious disease process is at work; why entertaining stressful thoughts and over-analyzing how to navigate life's "troubles" obscures one's connection with their innate resource of creativity and new thoughts (i.e., insights); why, when people think they are responsible for other people's feelings, this thinking places them in a resistive process that can break them down; and the distinction between tiredness as a feeling and energy production as a biological process that is managed by Universal Mind.

Weekly Webinars

Participants attended 90-minute weekly webinars facilitated by the 3P practitioners. Webinars were held three days after the release of each weekly video to allow time for participants to view and reflect on the video, complete the weekly reading assignment, and come to the webinars with questions and concerns.

Facebook Group

The Facebook group served to continue the conversation with and between participants outside the main education components. It was also used to post quotes, blogs, and videos from other 3P practitioners as well as a source for participants to share queries, reflections, success stories, and new insights.

Individual Coaching

Each participant had 1-2 individual coaching sessions (via Skype) with a 3P facilitator to explore certain topics more deeply and privately. Each coaching session was approximately 60 minutes.

The Results

Compared with the waitlist control group, participants receiving 3P education reported a significant increase in psychological and physical wellbeing and a significant decrease in depression, anxiety, fatigue, and pain interference. After receiving this education, waitlist control participants also reported a significant increase in psychological and physical wellbeing and a significant decrease in anxiety, fatigue, and pain interference. The significant improvements reported by participants in both experimental groups were maintained at a 6-month follow-up.

Participants in both experimental groups also responded to the following qualitative item, "Please compare the results you experienced from 3P mental health education with the results you may have experienced from other CFS interventions." Some responses follow:

- "I've engaged in various therapies including talking therapies, counseling, and graded exercise therapy, to name a few. This program has differed because instead of creating more thinking it has opened up opportunities to experience a calm, quiet mind. It's also taught me that I don't need to be on a quest in my life to be ok and I don't need to do anything when I'm experiencing symptoms. I don't need to get rid of them or fix myself. The diagnosis, the label, the treatment, it all adds to more thinking, and more resistance."

- "I do view CFS/ME differently. I knew in theory that I was creating it in my mind but could not see what to do with that information to feel better. The insights I gained on this program helped me understand more deeply how it is 100% created in the mind. I now understand the psychology and biology connection and see how my chronic overthinking created my symptoms."

- "This program has allowed me to change not just my views and thinking towards ME but my life and deepened my understanding of the human body and mind. I now feel that ME is definitely able to be "cured" and controlled through controlling our overthinking and there is a link between the patterns of symptoms and our racing thoughts and mind."

- "I have been told over the past three years to monitor, check, pace, take it easy, go slow and do everything in my power not to have a relapse! For this study I was NOT told to do anything from the list above! How thankful and grateful I am for this study as I feel plugged back in and my spark is back! I do NOT think about ME anymore and before this study ME is mainly what I thought about!"

- "I view it (ME) completely differently now. The initial illness was real, but the last 3 years of illness was mostly a revved up nervous system, combined with trying so desperately hard to manage my life and illness. Living in constant fear, stress and tension only exacerbated my symptoms."

- "Before this program I saw CFS as a life sentence, I saw it as a solid thing that is impacting a quality of my life. I understand now that what is stopping me to do things is my thinking and not the feeling of tiredness. I also came to understand that if I listen to my body and don't push myself, I will be able to do more and more things without constantly saying to myself that "I am tired, I can't do this." I can clearly see that the fatigue is not a solid thing, I see it as a feeling of tiredness that can come and go without me being attached to it."

A DEEPER DIVE

On YouTube watch:

What is Health? A Conversation with John El-Mokadem

Bill and Linda Pettit – The Mind Body Phenomenon

The Three Principles and Physical, Emotional, and Spiritual Healing

Eating Disorders

The Problem

Eating disorders are some of the most difficult psychiatric disorders to treat and are associated with high rates of mortality, disability, and poor motivation for change. Psychological therapies, including CBT, are the first-line treatment. Yet, on average, the outcome of CBT and other treatments are typically poor, drop-out rates are high, and the evidence base is limited. Three Principles psychoeducation offers an alternative intervention that can be delivered in a group setting and attempts to engage participants' innate capacity for well-being and resilience.

Supportive Research

I participated in another study that examined the efficacy of Three Principles mental health education for people diagnosed with an eating disorder (e.g., anorexia nervosa, bulimia nervosa). This study was published in the *Journal of Spiritual Psychology and Counseling* (Franklin-Smith, Parker, Jones, Kelley, Sharma, Skidmore, & Felix, 2022). In this study, Three Principles education was referred to as Health Realization/Innate Health (or HR/IH). Below is a summary of this study.

Methods

Eight female participants referred by the Connect Eating Disorders Service in the U.K. attended a 15 session Three Principles psychoeducational group facilitated by two Three Principles trained therapists. Standard general psychiatric and eating disorders clinical outcome measures were administered immediately before and after the group, and pre-and-post group quantitative data were compared. Qualitative feedback data was also gathered using a feedback questionnaire carried out by one of the therapists immediately following the group.

The Results

All eight participants had a diagnosis of anorexia nervosa, and all completed the Three Principles intervention. A comparison of pre-and-post group data indicated a statistically significant improvement in the participants' weight, body mass index (BMI), and mean scores on the Eating Disorder Examination Questionnaire. Clinically significant positive changes were also noted for Rosenberg's Self-Esteem Scale, the Clinical Outcomes in Routine Evaluation scale, and the Eating Disorders Quality of Life Scale. The Three Principles education also demonstrated high levels of participant and carer satisfaction and acceptability.

Conclusion

The Three Principles psychoeducational approach warrants further study as a brief intervention for adults with eating disorders.

A DEEPER DIVE

On YouTube watch:

Thoughts that Make You Go Ugh: Eating Disorders Coaching for Recovery

The Three Principles for Eating Disorders and Low Self-Esteem: Ann Curtis

Eating Disorders Cure: Ann Curtis

Joe Bailey: Relapse, Insights, and Serenity

Neurodiversity Parts 1, 2, 3 & Part 4 with Elizabeth Lovius

Bill and Linda Pettit – The Mind Body Phenomenon

3PGC A Sleeper's Dream: The Cure for Insomnia with Jen Lucas

3PGC Beauty in Ugly Places: What Alzheimers Showed Me about the Principles with Brianne Grebil

Bruce Lipton Ph.D. - The Power of Our Mind and How Fear and Stress Compromise Our Health

PART VII

When Mainstream Psychology Understands The Three Principles

CHAPTER 16

Flourishing Mental Health

Over a quarter century has passed since the first seeds of positive psychology were sewn by Mihalyi Csikszentmihalyi's research on creativity and "flow," Martin Seligman's work on learned optimism, Daniel Goleman's writings on emotional intelligence, Edward Deiner's work on subjective well-being, and David Myers's research on happiness. Since its christening in 2000, positive psychology has burgeoned. Contributors have constructed new theoretical models to better understand human strength and virtue, determine the well-springs, processes and mechanisms that lead to desirable consequences, and uncover the conditions and processes that contribute to flourishing mental health. Thousands of papers have been published in peer-reviewed journals on topics such as happiness, well-being, resilience, mindfulness, flow, and the relationship of these positive attributes with mental and physical health.

How much progress has positive psychology made toward meeting its primary goal of understanding and facilitating *optimal or flourishing* mental health? One estimate can be gleaned from the research of psychologist Corey Keyes, a prominent contributor to positive psychology. Keyes has written extensively about optimal mental health which he refers to as "complete" or "flourishing." Keyes operationalized mental health as "a syndrome of symptoms of positive feelings and positive functioning in life" which includes clusters of "symptoms" in three areas: *hedonic or emotional well-being* (e.g., positive affect, life satisfaction); *eudaimonic or psychological well-being* (e.g., autonomy, self-acceptance); and *social well-being* (e.g., social interaction, social actualization). Keyes posited that people who typically experience well-being in each of these areas are "flourishing" and "…anything less than flourishing is associated with increased impairment, disability, and burden to self and society." Keyes concluded that only a small portion of adults (free of a common mental disorder) experience flourishing mental health—that the prevalence of "flourishing" is less than 20% of the adult population! While around 50% of adults have moderate mental health, Keyes asserted that flourishing people function markedly better than all others:

> "…flourishing—reported …the healthiest psychosocial functioning (i.e., low helplessness, clear goals in life, high resilience, and high intimacy), the lowest risk of cardiovascular disease, the lowest number of chronic physical diseases, the fewest health limitations of activities of daily living, and lower health care utilization. However, the prevalence of flourishing is barely 20% of the adult population … only 17% of adults are completely mentally healthy."

Keyes highlighted two factors that he posited have prevented positive psychology from achieving the goal of understanding and facilitating flourishing mental health. First, he faulted funding agencies such as the National Institute of Mental Health and the Substance Abuse and Mental Health Services Administration for focusing mainly on remedial psychotherapy research and services. Second, he criticized the reactive orientation of mainstream psychology and called for a more proactive approach to mental health care to determine "…the earliest deviations from health… so as to intervene at the earliest stage and restore health rather than wait to manage chronic illness."

Promoting flourishing mental health should be the primary goal of mainstream psychology and mainstream psychology is far from achieving this goal. However, while increased national funding for mental health research and a more proactive approach to mental health care are clearly warranted, something more essential is needed for mainstream psychology to understand the true source of flourishing and how to best promote it—*a sufficient understanding, via insight, and adoption of the Three Principles.* Absent Universal Principles that synthesize the positive and the negative and unite different conceptions of the positive and the good, mainstream psychology will never achieve this goal. *Only after mainstream psychology realizes, understands, and adopts the Principles of Universal Mind, Consciousness, and Thought, will mental ill-health plummet and the percentage of people who are flourishing dramatically increase!*

Supportive Research

Jack Pransky, Eric Lambert, and I conducted a study that examined the relationship between understanding the Principles of Universal Mind, Consciousness, and Thought and flourishing mental health *as defined and measured by Corey Keyes.* Our study was published in the *Journal of Spirituality in Mental Health* (Kelley, Pransky, & Lambert, 2016). A summary of our findings follows.

The Participants

Organizations that teach the Three Principles sent electronic requests to their current and former students, directing them to the survey site. One hundred ninety-six people completed the survey. Approximately 63% were female and 86% were White. The mean age was 51 and the age range was 23 to 82. On average, participants were first exposed to the Three Principles 9.75 years before completing the survey. Most participants reported a moderate to high level of understanding of the Three Principles.

The Results

The results supported our hypotheses that participants' understanding of the power of Thought and the power of innate mental health will show a significant positive relationship with emotional well-being, psychological well-being, social well-being, and flourishing mental health. The most noteworthy finding of our study was—*88% of the participants exposed to Three Principles mental health education self-reported as "flourishing!* This finding is striking when compared to those of considerable mental health research that, on average, *the percentage of people in the U.S., the U.K., and several other developed countries diagnosed as flourishing ranges from 14-18%!*

A DEEPER DIVE

On YouTube watch:

3PGC--Falling in Love with Life with Semantha Hurst

3PGC – Moving from Ego to Essence, How to Thrive in a World Addicted to Fear with Jacquie Ford

PODCAST:

Psychology Has It Backwards, Episode #63—Toxic Positivity

CHAPTER 17

The Future of Mainstream Psychology

The Three Principles "inside-out/nothing-missing" paradigm is typically seen by mainstream psychology as a theory, philosophy, or model grounded in or derived from other psychological, spiritual, or psycho-spiritual perspectives (e.g., cognitive-behavioral, emotional, interpersonal, neurobiological, biopsychosocial, Buddhist). It is both common and expected that new approaches draw from, ground themselves in, and build upon previously existing theories and philosophies. However, the Three Principles understanding is not meant to be viewed as a theory or philosophy, nor is this understanding (or its intervention) meant to be seen as derived from other theories or philosophies. Rather, the Three Principles are meant to represent psycho-spiritual facts—*the essence or core of everything, including all theories, philosophies, and interventions.* Although mainstream psychology may dispute Banks's notion of how these Principles work together as theory, it would have to be using these very Principles to do so! In their groundbreaking book, *Sanity, Insanity, and Common Sense,* Rick Suarez, Roger Mills, and Darlene Stewart put it this way:

> "A cardinal aspect of the Three Principles understanding is that it clarifies how, in the absence of [a sufficient] understanding of the power of [the Three Principles] psychology has become stuck within the confines of problem-oriented ways of seeing reality

without knowing they are experiencing the end products of their own thinking. The intervals between great discoveries or changes are characterized by a growing dependence on certain fixed ideas and views, in a manner that inhibits change. As a result, humanity has periodically had to struggle to free itself from its own outdated ideas in order to advance its understanding. In this respect, [mainstream] psychology has been no different in terms of the maze of theories through which it attempts to help people."

Mainstream psychology has developed myriad theoretical formulations which relate mental ill-health and mental health with arbitrary variables it views as significant. Following this, mainstream psychologists spend their lives and careers focusing on these variables in their research, teaching, policies, interventions, and programming. Unfortunately, this process, while often dedicated and intellectually satisfying, has not produced the results or breakthroughs that mainstream psychology has envisioned. While mainstream psychology continues daily to add to the mountain of studies and descriptive details of every possible kind and type of mental ill-health that exists, the answers and results it seeks remain elusive. Mainstream psychology must begin to comprehend that its prevailing theories regarding mental health and mental ill-health are flawed and biased because they flow directly from the conditioned separate realities of their formulators. Absent this awareness, mainstream psychology will continue to add more confusion, complexity, and diversity to the field because it will continue, unknowingly, to be at the mercy of these conditioned separate realities.

The logic of the Three Principles reveals that it is no longer plausible to look at outside forces or external conditions as the source of either psychological dysfunction or mental well-being. The logic of the Three Principles turns cause and effect inside-out. For example, the sources of mental well-being posited by positive psychology (e.g., supportive friendships, challenging work, religious faith, intimate marriages, realistic goals, etc., etc.) *turn out to be effects, not causes*! The Principles of

Universal Mind, Consciousness, and Thought reveal only one source of people's psychological experiences (dysfunctional to optimal)—*the use of the Power to create thoughts brought to life by the power to have a sensory experience of those thoughts.*

A sufficient insight-based understanding of the Three Principles can move mainstream psychology to a deeper, more precise understanding of the way people's psychological lives are created, turning attention away from the illusion of external causes and focusing instead on the way everyone's psychological experiences are created from the "inside-out" via their use of the Three Principles. Only two ways of being are possible for everyone at any given time. Either they are operating from wisdom, peace of mind, well-being, and love—which "appear" naturally whenever they fall into the present moment and the default setting of innate mental health (i.e., Universal Mind) engages—or this innate health/wisdom is being overridden by personal thinking that is not serving them well. The Three Principles demonstrate how everyone can access and operate from innate well-being and wisdom throughout life because this health is their natural state, a state that comes through consciousness uncontaminated by personal thoughts.

There exists the tendency of any organized body of knowledge to keep going over old ground and accept only that which can be re-cognized within the limits of those definitions, concepts, interpretations, and expectations. Thus, the search for new or unknown knowledge often becomes re-search at a previously established level of understanding. Again, in the words of Rick Suarez, Roger Mills, and Darlene Stewart:

> "… It is often said that one of the things we have learned from history is that we have not learned from history. One of the things that the history of science is replete with is that the most difficult thing to recognize is new knowledge."

On the other hand, to the degree that mainstream psychology has the humility to step back from its adherence to its cherished points of view, it will see a larger picture and begin to gain insight into the power and validity of the Principles of Universal Mind, Consciousness, and Thought. Mainstream psychology will then see how these three psycho-spiritual Principles precisely connect the variables of thought, perception, motivation, emotion, and behavior. It will realize that the simplicity of these Three Principles gives psychology the means to generate a powerful, consistent, common-sense approach to halt the striking rise in mental ill-health and dramatically increase the number of people who self-report as flourishing. Amit Sood, also known as the "Ultimate Happiness Doctor," stated:

> "When science has matched spirituality, it creates a milieu for transformation. This is… timeless wisdom that sages have told us, that scientists are finding. Science is nothing but the study of spirituality… [and] science doesn't know it. Science will know it at some point. I believe this is what the children of the world need. They want us adults to be grateful, to be compassionate, to be accepting, to live our lives with meaning and have forgiveness. And if we do that, we will create a wonderful world for them."

At the point in time when mainstream psychology becomes conscious of the power and utility of the psycho-spiritual Principles of Universal Mind, Universal Consciousness, and Universal Thought, it will break through to a scientific discipline capable of producing unequivocal generalizations, generating consistent policies that make sense, and implementing mental health education with the power to make reducing mental ill-health and increasing flourishing an idea whose time has come. Sydney Banks summed it up as follows:

> "…the understanding of the Three Principles is both a cure and a prevention for the errors that occur in the human thought system… They are the missing link that changes psychology from a philosophy into a working science."

A DEEPER DIVE

On YouTube watch:

The Secret of Everything with Sydney Banks

Remap Your Psychology with Dicken Bettinger

Jamie Smart – The Three Principles: Future of Psychology

3PGC The Profound Simplicity of Mental Health with Dr. Mark Howard

Afterword

The end of our journey is at hand. Thank you for allowing me to introduce you to your true self—**the Three Principles in action!** Via a sufficient understanding of the Three Principles, people's lives show up as precious gifts to be savored and appreciated—the scent of lilacs in the spring—the smell of burning leaves on a crisp fall day—the touch of a friend's hand on your shoulder—an ice cream cone—a gentle breeze—a kiss on the cheek from a small child. The value of understanding the Three Principles for individuals, couples, families, educators, psychologists, organizations, and nations is incalculable. As more and more people grasp the Three Principles, the power of Thought, and the power of innate mental health, the possibility of "a world that works for everyone" will transform into "a reality whose time has come." Through the new insights you have gained on our journey together, you are creating that future now!

Love, Tom

APPENDIX 1

Three Principles Papers, Chapters, And Comments Published in Peer Refereed Academic & Professional Journals, Books, and Periodicals (1988-2022)

Kelley, T. M. & Manning, K. (2022). Realizing the power of Thought and innate mental health: Two overlooked ingredients for resolving traumatic memories. *Journal of Spirituality in Mental Health.*

Felix, F., Franklin-Smith, M., Rys Jones, W., Kelley, T. M., Parker, S., Sharma, V., & Skidmore, C. (2022). The efficacy of Health Realization/ Innate Health psychoeducation for individuals with eating disorders: Pilot study. *Spiritual Psychology and Counseling.*

Marshall, K. (2022). Discovering resilience and well-being in school communities. In L. Nabors (Ed.), *Resilient children, Springer series on child and family studies.*

Kelley, T. M., Pettit, W. F., Sedgeman, J. A., & Pransky, J. B. (2021). One generic mental illness: A psycho-spiritual explanation of general factor p and its application to clinical practice. *Spiritual Psychology and Counseling*, 6(2), 7-26.

Kelley, T. M., Wheeldon-Reece, B., & Lambert, E. (2021). The efficacy of mental health education for improving the mental health and school climate perceptions for students at risk for school failure. *Spiritual Psychology and Counseling*, 6(2), 73-93.

Green, A. L., Ferrante, S., Boaz, T. L. *et al.* (2021). Evaluation of the SPARK child mentoring program: A social and emotional learning curriculum for elementary school students. *Journal of Primary Prevention*, 42(5), 531-547.

Green, A. L., Ferrante, S., Boaz, T. L., & Wheeldon-Reece, B. (2021). Social and emotional learning during early adolescence: Effectiveness of a classroom based SEL program for middle school students. *Psychology in the Schools*, 58(6), 1056-1069.

Kelley, T. M., Kessel, A., Collings, R., Rubinstein, B., Monnickendam, C., & Solomon, A. (2021). Evaluation of the iHEART mental health education programme on resilience and wellbeing of U.K. secondary school adolescents. *Journal of Public Mental Health*. DOI: 10.1108/ JPMH-03-2020-0019.

Kelley, T. M., Pettit, W. F., Sedgeman, J. A,. & Pransky, J. B. (2020). Psychiatry's pursuit of euthymia: Another wild goose chase or an opportunity for Principle-based facilitation? *International Journal of Psychiatry in Clinical Practice*. DOI: 10.1080/13651501.2020.1837182.

El-Mokadem, J., DiMarko, K., Kelley, T. M., & Duffield, L. (2020). Three Principles/Innate Health: The efficacy of a new mental health education intervention for chronic fatigue syndrome. *Spirituality in Clinical Practice*. DOI:10.1037/scp0000232.

Kelley, T. M., Pettit, W. F., Pransky, J., & Sedgeman, J. (2019). A new "inside-out" view of general factor p. *European Psychiatry*, 61, 85-87.

Kelley, T. M., Hollows, J., Savard, D., & Pransky, J. (2019). The efficacy of intensive three principles correctional counseling for improving the mental health/resilience of people in an English prison. *Offender Rehabilitation,* 58(8), 661-677.

Kelley, T. M., & Pransky, J. (2018) A new principle-based view of intimate partner violence and its prevention. *Partner Abuse,* 9, 1, 58-74.

Evans, D. R., & Pevalin, D. J. (2017). Using the principle-based model to improve well-being in school: A mixed-methods pilot study. *Sage Open,* DOI: 10.1177/2158244017716217.

Kessel A., Neil, M., Marmer, E., & Malik, R. (2017). A superpower? An educational initiative? Or something else ... *Journal of Public Mental Health,* 16(4), 169-171.

Kelley, T. M., Hollows, J., Lambert, E. G., Savard, D., & Pransky, J. (2017). Teaching health vs. treating dysfunction: The efficacy of three principles correctional counseling with residents in an English prison. *International Journal of Offender Therapy and Comparative Criminology,* 62(9), 2831-2856.

Pransky, J., & Kelley, T. M. (2017). How the formless comes into form: A process by which Universal Mind powers Consciousness and Thought to create people's psychological lives. *Cogent Psychology,* DOI:10.1080/23311908.2017. 1307633.

Kelley, T. M., Alexander, J., & Pransky, J. (2017). Drawing-out inner resilience in children and high-risk adolescents via exposing them to three psycho-spiritual principles. *Journal of Child and Adolescent Behaviour,* 5(2), DOI: 10.4172/2375-4494.1000343.

Kelley, T. M., Pransky, J., & Lambert, E. A. (2016). Realizing improved mindfulness/flow/mental health through understanding three spiritual principles. *Journal of Spirituality in Mental Health,* 19(2), 133-150.

Kelley, T. M., Pransky, J., & Lambert, E. A. (2016) Understanding spiritual principles or using techniques to realize and sustain optimal mental health. *Journal of Spirituality in* Mental Health, 18(3), 217-238.

Kelley, T. M., Pransky, J., & Lambert, E. A. (2015). Realizing improved mental health through understanding three spiritual principles. *Spirituality in Clinical Practice*, 2(4), 267-281.

Kelley, T. M., Pransky, J. & Lambert, E. A. (2015). Inside-out or outside-in: Understanding spiritual principles versus depending on techniques to realize improved mindfulness/mental health. *Journal of Spirituality in Mental Health* 17(3), 153-171.

Kelley, T. M., Pransky, J., & Sedgeman, J. (2014). Realizing resilience in trauma exposed juvenile offenders: A promising new intervention for juvenile justice professionals. *Journal of Child and Adolescent Trauma*, 7, 143-151.

Pransky, J., & Kelley, T. M. (2014). Three principles for realizing mental health: A new psycho-spiritual view. *Journal of Creativity in Mental Health*, 9, 53-68.

Kelley, T. M., and Pransky, J. (2013). Principles for realizing resilience: A new view of trauma and human resilience. *Journal of Traumatic Stress Disorders and Treatment*, 2, 1, doi.org/10.4172/2324-8947.1000102.

Kelley, T. M. (2011) Thought recognition and psychological well-being: An empirical test of principle-based correctional counselling, *Counselling and Psychotherapy Research*, 11(2), 140-147.

Kelley, T. M., & Lambert, E. A. (2012). Mindfulness as a potential means of attenuating anger and aggression for prospective criminal justice professionals. *Mindfulness. 3(4), 261-274.*

Halcon, L. L., Robertson, C. L., & Monsen, K. A. (2010). Evaluating health realization for coping among refugee women. *Journal of Loss and Trauma, 15,* 408-425.

Kelley, T. M. (2008). Principle-based correctional counseling: Teaching health versus treating illness. *Applied Psychology in Criminal Justice.* 4 (2), 182-202.

Banerjee, K., Howard, M., Manheim, K., & Beattie, M. (2007). Comparison of health realization and 12-step treatment in women's residential substance abuse treatment programs. *American Journal of Drug and Alcohol Abuse, 33*, 207-215.

Halcon, L. L., Robertson, C. L., Monson, K. A., & Claypatch, C. C. (2007). A theoretical framework for using health realization to reduce stress and improve coping in refugee communities. *Journal of Holistic Nursing*, 25(3), 186-94.

Sedgeman, J. A., & Sarwari, A. (2006). The effect of a health realization/innate health psychoeducational seminar on stress and anxiety in HIV-positive patients. *Medical Science Monitor*, 12(10), 397–399.

Sedgeman, J. A. (2005). Health realization/innate health: Can a quiet mind and positive feeling state be accessible over the lifespan without stress relief techniques? *Medical Science Monitor*, 11, 47 –52.

Kelley, T. M. (2005). Mental health and prospective police professionals. *Policing*. 4, 1, 6-27.

Kelley, T. M. (2004). Positive psychology and adolescent mental health: False promise or true breakthrough? *Adolescence*. 39, 154, 257-278.

Kelley, T. M. (2003). Preventing youth violence through Health Realization. *Youth Violence and Juvenile Justice*. 1, 4, 369-387.

Kelley, T. M. (2003). Health Realization: A Principle-based psychology of positive youth development. *Child and Youth Care Forum*. 1, 47-72.

Kelley, T. M., & Stack, S. A. (2000). Thought recognition, locus of control, and adolescent well-being. *Adolescence*. 25, 139, 531-550.

Kelley, T. M. (2014). Happiness versus genuine mental health. (Comment) *Psychotherapy Networker*.

Kelley, T. M. (2015). Resolving trauma via thought recognition. (Comment) *Psychotherapy Networker.*

Kelley, T. M., Pransky, J, & Lambert, E. (2016). Realizing improved mental health through understanding three spiritual principles. *Research Review: A Digest of New Scientific Research Concerning Religion, Brain, and Behavior.* Joel Daniels (Ed.) Institute for the Bio-Cultural Study of Religion (IBCSR).

Kelley, T. M. (2017). The bewildering world of therapeutic aps. (Comment) *Psychotherapy Networker.*

Kelley, T. M. (2017). The hidden troublemaker in every relationship. In L. Carpanos & C. Heath (Eds.) (pp. 92-95). *The secret of love: Unlock the mystery, unleash the magic.* Edmonton: Canada, Three Principles Publishing.

Kelley, T. M. (2005). Natural resilience and innate mental health. *American Psychologist,* 56, 1, 36-37. *American Psychologist.* 60, 3, 265.

Kelley, T. M. (2001). The need for a principle-based positive psychology. *American Psychologist,* 56, 1, 36-37.

Kelley, T. M. (1996). A critique of social bonding and control theory of delinquency using the principles of Psychology of Mind. *Adolescence.* 31, 122, 321-327.

Kelley, T. M. (1993). Neo-cognitive learning theory: Implications for prevention and early intervention strategies with at-risk youth. *Adolescence.* 28, 110, 439-460.

Kelley, T. M. (1993). An advanced criminology based on Psychology of Mind. *Offender Rehabilitation.* 19, 173-190.

Kelley, T. M. (1993). Crime and Psychology of Mind: A neo-cognitive view of delinquency. In G. Barak (Ed.) *Varieties of Criminology: Readings from a Dynamic Discipline.* Praeger.

Kelley, T. M. (1990). A neo-cognitive model of crime. *Offender Rehabilitation.* 16, 1-26.

Mills, R., Dunham, R., & Alpert, G. (1988). Working with high-risk youth in prevention and early intervention programs: Toward a comprehensive wellness model. *Adolescence,* 23(91), 643-660.

Sydney Banks's Books, Audios, and Videos

Sydney Banks newly edited and released—videotaped before his death: https://3pgc.org/new-sydney-banks-videos/

Sydney Banks original web site: https://sydneybanks.org/

Find Books, Audios and Videos by Sydney Banks here: http://sydbanks.com/

Sydney Banks: A Collection of Four Vintage Recordings: https://3pgc.org/product/sydney-banks-a-collection-of-four-vintage-recordings/

Additional Sydney Banks videos: https://3pgc.org/videos-sydney-banks/

Please take time to enjoy the more than 150 recorded webinars on the 3PGC YouTube Channel.

Three Principles Books, Blogs, Podcasts and More!

Books: https://3pgc.org/practitioner-books/

Blogs: https://3pgc.org/practitioner-blogs/

Podcasts: https://3pgc.org/practitioner-podcasts/

YouTube Channels: https://3pgc.org/practitioner-youtube-channels

About the Author

Dr. Tom Kelley is an Emeritus Professor in the Department of Criminology and Criminal Justice at Wayne State University in Detroit, Michigan. Tom is also a Licensed Clinical Psychologist at Reflections Counseling Center in Troy, Michigan, and an internationally known researcher and mental health educator. Tom has authored over 100 empirical studies, papers, chapters, and comments published in peer-refereed academic and professional journals, books, and periodicals. Over 40 of Tom's publications are grounded in the psycho-spiritual Principles of Universal Mind, Consciousness, and Thought uncovered by Mr. Sydney Banks. Tom has also written two Three Principles-based books—*Falling in Love with Life* and *How Good Can You Stand It?* In his university classes, trainings, and private practice, Tom has assisted thousands of people to understand the way the Principles of Universal Mind, Consciousness, and Thought manifest within everyone to create their psychological lives.

Acknowledgments

For several decades I searched for more happiness, well-being, and peace of mind. Finally, via grasping a sufficient insight-based understanding of three Universal Principles—Universal Mind, Universal Consciousness, and Universal Thought—I realized the way to more contentment, vitality, and well-being than I ever thought possible! Writing this book was a labor of love. I want to acknowledge some beautiful people who assisted me on my journey.

- Mr. Sydney Banks for uncovering the Three Principles and the passion and courage to share this undersatanding with the world.

- Roger Mills and George Pransky for the humility and wisdom to quiet their egos, realize the power of this understanding, and assist Mr. Banks to introduce the world to the Three Principles.

- Rick Suarez, Roger Mills, and Darlene Stewart for their groundbreaking book, Sanity, Insanity, and Common Sense, which was my first exposure to several new understandings that eventually became known as the Three Principles.

- The following wonderful colleagues and friends for their wise words and writings that helped deepen my (and countless others) understanding of the Three Principles. Jack Pransky, Bill & Linda Pettit, George & Linda Pransky, Judy Sedgeman, Christine Heath, Roger & Clytee Mills, Dicken & Cozie Bettinger, Ken Manning, Joe Bailey, Mark Howard, Sandy Krot, Jeff Timm, Annika Hurwitt, Jacquie Ford, John El-Mokadem, Gordan Trockman, Cathy

Casey, Keith Blevens, Jacqueline Hollows, Carol Ringold, Rita Shuford, Rudi and Jules Kennard, Linda Ramos, Kathy Marshall, Joe Boyle, Michael Neil, Rohini Ross, Valda Monroe, Rob Cook, Chantel Burns, Brooke Wheeldon-Reece, Elizabeth Lovius, Ami Johnson, and Ami Chen Mills.

- Roger Mills for his wise, kind, patient mentoring and the generous Foreword to this book.
- Bill Pettit, Judy Sedgeman, and Jack Pransky for their unrelenting commitment to the integrity of the Three Principles and their kind and generous support and guidance.
- My beautiful angels—Susan ("My Duck"), Marty, Kathy, Ricky, Faith, and Michael. Thank you for your unconditional love and support. I love you!